WELFARE AND WISDOM

WELFARE AND WISDOM

Edited by

JOHN S. MORGAN

Lectures delivered on the
Fiftieth Anniversary of the
School of Social Work of the
University of Toronto

UNIVERSITY OF TORONTO PRESS

Reprinted 1968
SBN 8020 5168 5
Printed in Belgium

Foreword

CHARLES E. HENDRY

THE PUBLICATION OF THIS BOOK is the culmination and climax of a celebration, the Fiftieth Anniversary of the University of Toronto graduate School of Social Work. Its theme, the meaning of welfare in the modern world, is in the tradition of Urwick, MacIver, and Cassidy, former directors of the School. Its format and pattern, interdisciplinary and international, emphasize its universal relevance and rationale.

Warm appreciation is expressed to the President of the University, Dr. Claude Bissell, for his personal and official interest and support. Dr. Bissell quickly sensed the timeliness and significance of the undertaking, in terms of both its substantive and its strategic importance.

My colleagues and I are grateful also to the Dean of the School of Graduate Studies, the heads of the departments of Sociology, Economics, Political Science, and Philosophy for their co-operation, the Dean and Director of the Faculty of Music and the Master of Massey College for their helpfulness in providing the MacMillan Theatre for the lectures and the Upper Library for the colloquia, the secretary of the School for her most effective supervision of the operation, and not least to the Director of the University of Toronto Press and the members of his staff who, in co-operation with Professor Morgan and Mrs. Florence Strakhovsky, edited, designed, and produced this commemorative volume.

Special thanks are reserved for Professor John Morgan, who has served as editor and who has written an interpretive and integrative essay by way of a formal introduction to the publication of the eight lectures. While his primary focus is on meanings and implications for Canada, the lectures themselves, as well as Professor Morgan's essay, go well beyond the provincialism of geography, the parochialism of institutions, and the professionalism of any profession. Our indebtedness to the four distinguished scholars who came to Toronto and who delivered the eight lectures here reproduced is beyond calculation. We trust that this Fiftieth Anniversary volume, *Welfare and Wisdom*, may provide perspective, incentive, and guidance in the development of humane and liberating social and economic policy. Our hope is that all who read this book will find in it a design for dignity.

CHARLES E. HENDRY
Director, School of Social Work
University of Toronto

September, 1965

Contents

FOREWORD by Charles E. Hendry   v

JOHN S. MORGAN

    Welfare and Wisdom: A Commentary   3

T. H. MARSHALL

    Welfare in the Context of Social Development   25

    Welfare in the Context of Social Policy   41

EUGEN PUSIĆ

    The Political Community and the Future of Welfare   61

MALCOLM S. ADISESHIAH

    Welfare in Economic Thought: Some Micro-
    Economic Propositions   97

    Welfare in Economic Action: Some Macro-
    Economic Conclusions   117

CHARLES FRANKEL

    The Moral Framework of the Idea of Welfare   147

    The Transformation of Welfare   165

JOHN S. MORGAN

Welfare and Wisdom:
A Commentary

JOHN S. MORGAN

Dean, School of Social Work,
University of Pennsylvania

Professor Morgan graduated in modern history at the University of
Oxford in 1932 and did graduate work in education at Armstrong
College, University of Durham (now the University of Newcastle upon
Tyne). He occupied positions with the Tyneside Council of Social Service
1933–36, and the National Council of Social Service (London, England)
1936–46, joining the faculty of the University of Toronto School of
Social Work in 1946. He has been Visiting Professor at the Universities
of Chicago and Manchester, McGill University and Columbia University
of New York; and became Dean of the School of Social Work, University
of Pennsylvania in 1967. He has served as consultant to the United
Nations and a number of governments in Europe and North America.
His publications include numerous studies of social policy and social
welfare administration.

Welfare and Wisdom:
A Commentary

WELFARE AS A PHENOMENON of paramount importance in the life of modern nations can easily be demonstrated. Each nation devotes annually a substantial amount of its Gross National Product to "health and welfare services." In immediate terms for Canadians, it is a striking fact that in the National Budget for 1965 the estimated expenditures on health and welfare exceed, for the first time, the estimated costs of national defence. Each of them has an expanding bureaucracy concerned with public service, absorbing and employing an increasing proportion of scarce resources of professional manpower, money, and material. Welfare as a social, economic, and political concept in the realm of ideas is much less pre-eminent than the volume and importance of the practical activities that are undertaken in its name.

But it is one of the paradoxes of modern nations that although they all allocate so significant a proportion of their Gross National Product to government expenditures on "health and welfare services" there is great confusion about the concepts of both health and welfare. While it is true that the World Health Organization has produced a general definition of health expressed in positive terms, the concept of health is still usually expressed in negative terms, as the absence of physical or mental abnormality. Almost without exception the so-called national health programmes are almost exclusively concerned with the cure of sickness and the correction of abnormal conditions, rather than with the preservation and enhancement of health. There is no comparable definition of welfare available, and welfare services are almost invariably perceived as being concerned with the alleviation of poverty and the correction of conditions of social deprivation.

In its institutions and in the ways in which it determines the use of its human and material resources, every human society gives expression to a number of general concepts, which are generally accepted in that society as fundamental values. Thus, for example, territorial domination was, for centuries, a measure of a nation's "greatness" and the defence of "national honour" was a measure of "glory" or national integrity. Or again, a determination to spread "the true faith" has, throughout recorded history, claimed untold treasure and uncounted numbers of lives from human societies in all parts of the world. The emergence, in the nineteenth century, and the pre-eminence in the twentieth century, of the idea of human welfare as a legitimate objective of national and international policy makes it essential that this concept should be examined with some care. This book is concerned with the exploration of the idea of welfare in the context of a rapidly changing technological society. The authors were charged with the task of probing the frontiers of knowledge, each from a different cultural background and each using the tools of investigation derived from a different intellectual discipline. The contributors have successfully resisted the temptation to indulge in semantic gymnastics and have attempted, each in his own way, to explore the largely unformulated ideas that appear to them to need clarification if the concept of welfare is to be relevant to the rapidly changing scene of today's world. Because it is exploratory in its purpose, the work does not attempt a definitive thesis. It does presume to illustrate and illuminate an idea.

The single most significant result of this extended probe is the agreement of all the authors that welfare as an expression of human aspirations and as a legitimate expectation of organized society must take a prominent place in the scale of objectives to whose achievement a significant proportion of the human and material resources of society may and should be devoted. Each author arrives at this conclusion by very different routes. Thus, Professor Marshall writes:

For in my estimation, welfare must be envisaged as an integral part of the whole apparatus that includes social security, education, public health, the medical services, factory legislation, the right to strike, and all the other rights and legitimate expectations which are attached to modern democratic citizenship.

Professor Pusić at one point says succinctly:

In becoming a generally accepted goal of society, welfare is thus the primary rational content of social action.

While Dr. Adiseshiah writes:

That at least is the moral of this discourse—that all economic thought originates in welfare and is in the end tested by its contribution to welfare.

Professor Frankel concludes his own redefinition of welfare with:

The transformed view of welfare I am describing would presumably have a number of general consequences. It would remove the stigma from welfare. It would transform welfare from a peripheral function at the fringes of society to the central object of organized social planning. And it would turn reflection away from the problem of helping those who cannot help themselves, and towards the problem of creating conditions in which fewer people will need others' help.

If these tentative essays have the effect of concentrating some of the best minds in the disciplines of sociology, political science, economics, and philosophy upon welfare as a central object of theoretical enquiry, the world of practical welfare should reap untold benefits. The relative absence of speculative thought and the lack of a solid theoretical framework hitherto have left welfare too much at the mercy of the makers and breakers of images.

Each reader will select his own emphasis among the many significant ideas and will find illumination and inspiration where they touch most closely upon his own experience or his own background of knowledge. In a very real way this array of perceptive tools must itself be a characteristic of any realistic assessment of welfare and the place of welfare in modern society; for it seems clear from the work of these authors that one's concept of welfare is a product in large part of one's own past and of the past of the cultural norms to which one is heir by birth, by experience, and by deliberate cultivation. The present essay reflects the interests of one Canadian concerned with those ideas that emerge from this exploration which appear to be of particular significance to Canada as touchstones for the future of welfare in this country and the kaleidoscope of change that now engages a developing industrial nation in a time of transition.

All of the contributors give special emphasis to the family as an integral unit of social organization and as an essential institution through which welfare is achieved. At one point in his study, Professor Marshall says:

Today, I suggest, we recognize three types of social service—the statutory, the voluntary, and the family, which is the original and basic one. And their integration into a single, complex but unified welfare system is the outstanding achievement of the modern world in this field of endeavour.

Professor Frankel has an echo of this idea in a long passage where he traces the tremendous impact on Western thought of the idea of individual responsibility and the obligation of the individual to provide for his own welfare out of the sweat of his own brow and the work of his own hands. He then adds that "despite all that the philosophy we have been describing did to make reward for individual work the basic element in what we mean by justice, recognition of the special claims of kinship and family always remained strong. Inheritance was never abolished."

This identification of the family as a critical element in the organization and operation of the welfare services is really quite a new phenomenon. It is, moreover, certainly not as widely accepted as Professor Marshall suggests. Most of the major welfare services in Canada tend to ignore the family as a functioning partner in welfare and to concentrate on the task of meeting the needs of individuals. The major income maintenance programmes, in Canada as elsewhere, are intended to provide substitute incomes to individuals who are out of work, or disabled, or otherwise unable to earn sufficient income. Since wages are paid to the individual in direct proportion to his contribution to the productive process,

substitute incomes in the form of unemployment insurance benefits, workmen's compensation, old-age benefits, and even public
assistance are calculated in terms of individual benefits. It is true
that the social obligations of some individuals to maintain their
families are acknowledged by additional supplements in many programmes, but the basic benefit scale in these programmes is not
conceived in terms of a family income. Child welfare services, as
their very name indicates, have been thought of for the past fifty
years primarily as services to and for individual children for whom
the community feels some responsibility rather than for the family
of which the child is a member. It is true that the theorists of
family allowances have argued that all welfare payments should
be made on the basis of family needs, but the amounts of the
allowances do not suggest any effective relationship between the
scales of benefit and any concept of a family income or an acceptable standard of living for a Canadian family.

Two major opportunities now occur in Canada for the adoption
of the family as a basic unit of welfare. The federal government has
announced its intention to introduce a Canada Assistance Plan to
replace the complex medley of categorical assistance programmes
currently in force to which the federal government contributes a
substantial part of the cost. It would be a significant contribution
to the advance of welfare if the basic criteria of need to be adopted
in the assistance benefits under the new programme were to be
based upon a carefully researched and systematically stated family
standard of living, below which no Canadian family should be
allowed to fall.

Child welfare legislation in Canada is undergoing extensive over-
haul. The studies and reports that have preceded revision of the
laws in the various provinces have all stressed the importance of
family life. They have all emphasized the central role which must
be filled by the family in the successful rearing and nurturing of
children; they have all indicated that those welfare services must
be expanded and strengthened which support the family and enable
it better to fulfil its role in an increasingly complex social order. It
remains to be seen whether the proposals of the various legislatures
reflect this renewed concern for the quality and stability of family
life.

The rediscovery of the importance of the family to the fabric of

society can be demonstrated in other ways. There is a rapidly growing field of literature covering almost every aspect of family life.
It is of more than passing significance that the province of Quebec
has renamed its Department of Public Welfare as the Department
of Family and Social Services. It is equally relevant to note that
the Governor-General of Canada and Madame Vanier convened
the Canadian Conference on the Family in 1964 and that the outcome of this national conference has been the foundation of the
Vanier Institute on the Family. It is to be hoped that this move will
lead to the expansion of fundamental research and systematic
enquiry that must be undertaken if Canada is to adopt the position
suggested by Professor Marshall that families are equal partners
with governments and voluntary agencies in the operation of the
welfare services.

One of Professor Pusić's major contributions to the discussion
lies in his rigorous examination of organization theory and its
application to welfare; and his development of a powerful case for
what he describes as a "new social process, which might tentatively
be called the process of social self-management." His argument is
that the growth and proliferation of specialist and professional
knowledge and skills render the prevailing models of hierarchical
organization no longer viable. He suggests that in welfare services
particularly it will be essential to develop a new form of structure:

The new structure starts from the individual specialist who is supposed
to know his function. . . . This basic element of the individual contribution is then integrated into progressively wider patterns, the basic unit
of integration being the work team. The work team does not detract in
any way from the professional autonomy of each of its members, but
it gives to each individual activity its social meaning.

Professor Pusić, in his proposal for the deconcentration of
administration, would appear at first sight to suggest a complete
reversal of recent trends in Canadian public welfare. Recent official
reports in New Brunswick, Manitoba, and Ontario have all recommended the concentration of welfare services in larger units of
administration. His proposal would also appear to deny to the
welfare services the benefits to be derived from the application of

modern electronic data processing devices, which permit the handling of large volumes of routine work with a speed and accuracy hitherto unattainable by manual methods.

Further examination of Professor Pusić's proposals, however, suggests that, far from impeding progress in the development of effective welfare administration, they offer new opportunities to create more effective services than now exist. They would certainly require drastic reorganization of the present patterns of organization and administration. But they could give an elasticity and quality that would enable the services to adjust to the infinite variety of human need in ways that cannot be achieved within the inherent rigidities of more orthodox hierarchical models. The new design would place a new dimension of responsibility upon all the professions—including social work—the implications of which need to be explored.

Curiously enough, none of the authors pays very much attention to the impact of automation on society and on the welfare services. Professor Pusić does point out that any administrative procedure that can be routinized can be transferred with much greater efficiency to data processing machines. Thousands of procedures of this type are carried out daily in the welfare services to establish eligibility and to calculate the amounts of financial benefits. The introduction of the Canada Pension Plan is contingent upon the use of automation, and one province after another is already engaged in the transfer of its routine operation to computers. One of the outstanding authorities on automation, Dr. Bernard J. Muller-Thym, on the basis of his analysis of the capabilities of computer technology, has, in fact, arrived at conclusions about the nature of organization which support Professor Pusić's proposals, in his case derived from an analysis of organization theory:

Automation will also have an impact on our forms of organization, on work structure, and on the institutions of authority and control within the organization itself. Here again, we have been operating for perhaps half a century on the basis of certain assumptions about the organization of work done by human beings. We have always assumed, for example, that there must be someone who is superior over workers, that everyone must have a boss. . . . As a result of these assumptions, we have inevitably created a management work structure illustrated by the classical organization chart—a structure that is pyramidal and many layered. As a business organized in this way grows larger and larger, not only does the base of the pyramid broaden, but the number of intermediate layers (consisting of supervisors and managers) is multiplied.

We are already, and we have been for some time, beyond the tolerable limits of inefficiency that result from running a business with this kind of organizational structure. . . .

We already have working models of the new kind of organizational structure that increasing complexity will require. If you were to diagram them, they would look somewhat like diagrams of the nervous system, or the kind of diagrams nuclear scientists make. We might consider the present-day organization chart as a two-dimensional Euclidean structure in which any increase in size automatically creates greater distances between the various points. The new type of organization, in contrast, exists in a kind of curved space, where points of competence mobilization, points of decision-making, and points of information management are so arrayed that one can go directly, or almost directly, from any action-taking, decision-making, information-handling point to any other point.[1]

In a word, modern computer technology would seem to call for the creation of Professor Pusić's work teams in order to exploit this new extension of human capabilities in the development of welfare.

It may well be that Canada offers a peculiarly favourable situation for the development of new patterns of organization that will take full advantage of the principle of deconcentration proposed by Professor Pusić. Provincial jurisdiction in the field of welfare, at present the object of determined self-realization by at least one province, offers an immediate opportunity for the maximum deconcentration of competence mobilization, decision-making, and information handling to the provinces. The release of the provinces, through the operations of the Canada Pension Plan, from a substantial part of the financial burdens now carried by them under the current assistance programmes, and the latent opportunities of a new approach to public assistance in the proposed Canada Assistance Plan, have created a fluid situation in which experiments could and should be made to bring new theory to the test of

[1]Bernard J. Muller-Thym, "The Real Meaning of Automation," an address before the International Chamber of Commerce in Paris (photostat, n.d.).

practice. Canada's political system requires its welfare programmes to be organized on a pluralistic rather than a hierarchical basis, and this may prove to be an opportunity rather than a barrier to the adoption of creative new forms of organization that the theorists have now exposed.

Professor Frankel attaches primary importance to the preservation and extension of the right of individuals to make their own choices:

The assumption that there will be choice, that a pluralistic society will exist and that individuals will have some opportunity to say "yes" or "no" where official notions of human welfare are concerned, is central to what I have said. The transformed concept of welfare thus retains an essential element of the older concept. Its heart is the right to choose. It merely goes further than the older concept in its concern for freedom. It proposes to ensure that the beneficiaries of welfare measures have not only the right but the intelligent power to choose. That, it seems to me, is what "welfare," in the end, is all about. It stands for the effort to create a society in which individuals will have significant choices, and will have sufficient knowledge and ability and resources so that, when they make the choices, they can reasonably be held responsible for what they have done.

In this he seems to echo something of Professor Marshall's earlier observation:

It is, I think, fair to say that, as affluence spreads downwards through society, there takes shape in the minds of those who join the ranks of the comfortably-off a picture of the kind of life they want to live—a picture that is complete, concrete, and realistic, because they are thinking about something that is within their reach.

Wherever Frankel and Marshall place their criteria of having "sufficient knowledge and ability and resources" to choose, or being "comfortably off," it seems clear that they are thinking of Western industrial societies with high standards of living and substantial margins of resources that permit individuals and communities to make choices. It is not so clear that "this is what welfare is all about" in those societies that do not have any margin of resources to permit choices, indeed whose margin of resources, as Dr. Adiseshiah demonstrates in his paper, are shrinking relatively not only to the affluent nations but even to their own growing disbalance between their human population and their capacity to maintain their present low standards of living. Perhaps to the prime value of choice should be added Dr. Adiseshiah's comment that account must be taken of:

the kind of dynamics of life and society which are not encompassed within the economists' universe of discourse. In the affluent societies, which Europe and North America represent, in this rich one-third of our world, is it really necessary to expend so much effort and concentrate so much of our attention on the examination and analysis of optima and preferred positions, which emerge from grubbing around at the margin. A rich society can only progress further through allowing for wastes in order that it may continue in its affluence. To such a society, equations, arrived at by squeezing out this and adding to that at the margin, are not of decisive importance, because it has passed beyond that particular point.

There seems to be a real dilemma hidden here that needs further exploration. One of the most significant phenomena of welfare in the nineteen-sixties in North America is the rediscovery of poverty. Although technology and organization have made it possible to expand the production of wealth on an unprecedented scale, the affluent societies have thus far failed to devise means to secure an equitable distribution of these new riches. As a result, even in the most highly developed countries, as high a proportion as 25 per cent of the population have no choice, and their children will have no choice, of the kind of life they will lead, or the standards of living at which they are compelled to survive. This is a situation of which the late Archbishop of Canterbury, William Temple, wrote in 1942:

Why should some of God's children have full opportunity to develop their capacities in freely-chosen occupations, while others are confined to a stunted form of existence, enslaved to types of labour which represent no personal choice but the sole opportunity offered? The Christian cannot ignore a challenge in the name of justice.[2]

2William Temple, *Christianity and the Social Order* (3rd ed.; London: S.C.M. Press, 1950), pp. 19–20.

So long as a condition of widespread poverty remains so insistent a feature of society, it is not possible to ignore it as a concomitant of welfare. This point was well made by Professor Marshall:

Recently I put this question to two or three people in charge of welfare services in various parts of England. "Is it true," I asked, "that poverty is now irrelevant to welfare service?" The reaction was much the same in each case—a slight pause, a reflective nod of the head, and—"Yes, I suppose so," and then quite firmly, "Yes, it is." The hesitation is natural, for the issue is not simple.

It would be absurd to deny that poverty is an important factor in most situations in which the need for welfare service arises. But it is not poverty in the old sense of destitution, but rather lack of financial means to cope with a difficult situation.

It is almost certainly correct to say that the welfare services cannot correct the economic and social imbalances that create poverty. To attempt to use welfare services to this end can only distort the services. As Marshall sees it, and the analysis of welfare in Western industrial society would seem to support his view, welfare service is a resource that should be available to every citizen to meet a specific need, and it should not be a condition of service that he be poor as well as in need of service. The conquest of poverty, whether it be within a nation or within the world community, is not primarily a matter for welfare services but one of economic and social planning. Only when it has been achieved can the individual victims begin to make valid choices for which they can be held responsible.

There is an added implication here of the utmost significance to the concept of welfare in a modern industrial society. If it is accepted that the only eligibility requirement for welfare service should be the need for service, then logically welfare services should be universally available. Professor Marshall illustrates this position by reference to the British Health Service. This position is of particular relevance when the service is one which requires the mobilization of resources that are beyond the capacity of the individual citizen, or which requires the deployment on some basis of priority of resources in money, manpower, or skills that are in short supply. Perhaps a classic example of this position is in relation to dental services. No country has enough dentists to provide adequate dental care for the whole population, and a decision must therefore be made to deploy the available resources of dental care not in relation to ability to pay, or in relation to consumer choice, or even in relation to the regulators of the market place, but in relation to the public interest. In practice in Great Britain, and in the recommendations of the Hall Royal Commission on Health Services for Canada, the decision is to concentrate on the dental needs of children. The reasons underlying this choice are self-evident. It has not yet been appreciated, however, that the overriding public interest will have to prevail over sectional interests in determining priorities in the use of other scarce manpower resources in, for example, the use of social workers, or psychiatrists. It also becomes a matter of the public interest to expand the supply of qualified manpower in the professions which the public interest determines to be of importance to the community, and if necessary, to devote public funds and priority in allocation of educational resources to this purpose. It will also be necessary to require the professions to modify their patterns of qualification and of professional practice to permit the training of new types of workers capable of undertaking tasks hitherto reserved to members of the professions.

The determination of the public interest is, in a democratic society, essentially a political process. Herein lie the seeds of conflict in the development of new welfare policies for the future. Hitherto the determination of priorities in welfare services in North America has been, at least in substantial measure, the result of a complex balance of forces in which the ability of the consumer to pay (for example, for psychiatric care), or the prestige and social power of the organization (for example, long established private social agencies), or in the political social status of the professional group providing the service (for example, the medical profession), have all been decisive factors. In order to ensure that the public interest prevails, it becomes inevitable that there will be increasing government intervention and control in the welfare services. It is this necessity for the subordination of sectional interests to the public interest that has created and will continue to create some of the fiercest controversy in the planning and development of health and welfare services.

The perceptive reader of the papers in this book will probably detect a marked difference between the assumptions of each of the authors about the role of government in welfare. On the one hand, Professor Pusić and Dr. Adiseshiah assume the primacy of public authorities in the determination of priorities and the direction of programmes; Professor Marshall joins the public authority, the private voluntary organization, and the family in an integrated partnership; and Professor Frankel places major emphasis on the freedom of the individual to make choices. He probably states as advanced a position as the North American social and political climate will currently accept when he writes: "Social needs exist which it is romantic to expect that private enterprise will or can serve. A reasonable balance between the public and private sectors is a prerequisite to the adequate recognition and satisfaction of such general social needs." These underlying assumptions need to be recognized, since they colour the perceptions and condition the usefulness of the contributions of other cultures to the development of welfare services in a particular country. As Sir Geoffrey Vickers put it, in a new and perceptive analysis of *The Art of Judgment*:

One constant trend runs through all these changes—the restriction of individual choice, expressed through the market and the corresponding enlargement of political choice as an arbiter of values and priorities. Some will regret this trend, as a shift from the firm ground of individual preference, mediated through a market to the shifting sands of sectional interest, mediated by warring pressure groups. Others will welcome it as a means to secure closer attention to the manifold aspects of the public interest, as distinct from those of the well- or ill-matched parties to a reciprocal transaction. Both views are valid and anyone able to apprehend the change with all its associated losses and gains will share both.[3]

[3]Sir Geoffrey Vickers, *The Art of Judgment: A Study of Policy Making* (New York: Basic Books, 1965), p. 133.

Implicit in the contributions of all four authors is the recognition that welfare is a moral concept. Professor Frankel makes this explicit when he writes:

Welfare, then, is a moral idea for which we have to take full responsibility. Neither God nor Nature nor Pure Reason nor the Market System will let us off the moral hook. . . . To be an advocate of "welfare," or to be the official, citizen, or beneficiary of a "welfare state," is to be implicated in decisions and policies that involve large judgments about the proper ends of life.

With the exception of Professor Frankel's closely argued humanistic stance it is not easily apparent from the papers what sources of moral criteria the authors themselves have assumed as the basis of their decisions or choices for the definition of welfare in so far as they require "large judgments about the proper ends of life."

Among the values that the Western world has assumed without question for the past century or more has been the pre-eminent value of work. Work has been the criterion upon which individuals were paid an income. A willingness to and a capacity for work have been the hallmark of a good citizen. For a long time willingness to work was a test, and it still is a major test, of eligibility for welfare services.

Not all societies have accorded the same primacy of value to work, as was illustrated by Dr. Adiseshiah's humorous anecdote about the society in which it was said, "If ever the urge to work comes over you, just lie down and the feeling will pass away." It now appears to be at least possible, as a result of technological change, that work may lose its primacy in the hierarchy of values. The implications of this change are at present unknown. Dr. Muller-Thym has this to say about work:

But no amount of retraining is going to provide the amount of work that human beings now perform as sources of power, servo-mechanisms, levers, and things of this sort. No amount of work for human beings is going to replace the work that is being destroyed by automation.

In a world in which the prime mechanism for distributing the wealth we have learned to create has been pay for work, the disappearance of work has serious implications.[4]

Not all the authorities would go as far as Dr. Muller-Thym in suggesting that "no amount of work is going to replace the work that is being destroyed by automation." But the nature of work is certainly going to change. One aspect of technological development that has so far received too little attention is that the rapid changes in technology will alter the pattern of a "life's work" for most industrial workers, if they are to remain active members of the labour force. It is now generally accepted that a typical "work life" will require most workers to drop out of the labour market as their skills are rendered obsolete by technology and to undertake training for re-entry into the work force with newly acquired knowledge and skills. These periods of "non-work" seem likely to occur at intervals of ten to fifteen years. The social consequences of this pattern of work will be far-reaching both for the individual concerned and for the welfare services. The periods of non-work are likely to occur at critical periods in the worker's social life, for example just at the periods when he is faced with the major burdens of financing a home and rearing children and later when he would normally, under existing presumptions about career patterns, begin to save for retirement. If re-establishment in employment after a period of non-work (and retraining) involves the worker in dis-investment of home and savings, it will place further strains on the capacity of the most prudent individuals which they are unlikely to bear without substantial external help. If a lifetime of fluctuating income and social status is to become the normal pattern, welfare services like pension plans, health insurance, and income maintenance programmes will require extensive adaptation to the new situation. Education services will have to be expanded to span the lifetime of every citizen, and this will require the development of new methods of education appropriate to adult learning capacities, and a massive expansion and re-allocation of resources to the field of education.

[4]"The Real Meaning of Automation," an address before the International Chamber of Commerce in Paris (photostat, n.d.).

At least one of the implications of these impending changes in the nature of work is already to be seen in the widespread discussion now going on—simultaneously and independently—in both Europe and North America about the possibility of a guaranteed income as the cornerstone of welfare planning. The British government has announced, as a matter of basic policy, that it will attempt to establish a guaranteed income; the learned journals of social work, political science, and economics in North America have all published proposals that are variations on this theme; the publishers' lists begin to include scholarly studies aimed at the same objective. The fundamental idea is deceptively simple. Every citizen will each year make a declaration of income. Those whose incomes are "inadequate" will have their incomes made up to the guaranteed income from tax-funds raised by taxation of those whose incomes exceed the accepted level of "adequacy." The practical application of this concept poses complex and difficult problems, not the least of which is the problem of defining "income" in an economic world where credit over a lifetime and the power to purchase are the true tests of "wealth" rather than the cash available in a limited time period. These severe practical problems, however, are probably no more difficult of solution than the complexities of the organization of modern industry or the intricacies of international finance have been in the first half of the twentieth century. The significant fact is that sober and responsible people throughout modern society are turning their attention to the possibility of a guaranteed income for every citizen.

Revolutionary changes such as those suggested here in patterns of work and modes of income payment will not occur overnight. They are more likely to appear piecemeal—indeed they are already appearing—as responses to particular situations. Unless they are foreseen and the responses planned as rational steps on the path of change, they must inevitably produce both industrial confusion and much individual hardship. It therefore becomes imperative to develop social instruments and expand the range of research to provide sensitive and reliable long-range projections and appropriate plans for industrial and social change. The industrial revolution of the nineteenth century was paid for, in large part, by the squalor and deprivation that it imposed on the industrial worker and his family. There is no excuse for permitting the technological revolution of the twentieth century to take the price of change out of the lives of the many and leave the benefits in the hands of the affluent few. Welfare must be joined with economic and political planning if the lessons of the nineteenth century are not to be relearned at painful, and unnecessary, cost in the twentieth.

The direct implications of adopting a guaranteed incomes policy for welfare services have not yet received serious consideration. It would appear at least probable that such a policy would remove the necessity for "income maintenance programmes" from the arena of welfare. In Canadian terms, this would require the drastic amendment, if not the disappearance, of the Canada Pension Plan and the newly announced Canada Assistance Plan, in addition to unemployment insurance, workmen's compensation, family allowances and all the other federal and provincial programmes whose primary objective is to provide an income to individuals and families whose incomes derived from work are inadequate or non-existent. This would, in effect, remove perhaps 90 per cent of current government expenditures on "welfare" from the category of direct welfare services. The underlying concept of welfare would have to be broadened to cover services, such as housing, urban development, and leisure time occupations that provide the essential environment of an enhanced quality of living, as well as services, such as counselling, legal advice, or guidance in the management of credit that enable human beings to adjust effectively to human and social conditions with which they are confronted. The creation of these services would require a volume of research and planning and the education and training of qualified personnel for their operation on a scale that can hardly be comprehended as long as the main burden of welfare services is concentrated on income maintenance.

In a world in which welfare has been principally concerned with repairing—and occasionally preventing—the human damage to those who cannot work or who are deprived of work through no fault of their own, the dethronement of work and the income derived from work from the pinnacle of value criteria may have even more far-reaching consequences. It may sound romantic in 1965 to suggest that the "proper ends of life" to which welfare may legitimately adjust its values, should conform to Julian Huxley's recent statement in *Essays of a Humanist*:

The important ends of man's life include the creation and enjoyment of beauty, both natural and man-made; increased comprehension and a more assured sense of significance; the preservation of all sources of pure wonder and delight, like fine scenery, wild animals in freedom, or unspoiled nature; the attainment of inner peace and harmony; the feeling of active participation in embracing and enduring projects, including the cosmic project of evolution. It is through such things that individuals attain greater fulfilment. As for nations and societies, they are remembered not for their wealth or comforts or technologies, but for their great buildings and works of art, their achievements in science or law or political philosophy, their success in liberating human life from the shackles of fear and ignorance.[5]

It may sound romantic, but a more careful examination will suggest that this is precisely one of the directions in which welfare in the Western world is now moving. An increasing variety of occupations are now recognized as work which in an earlier age would not have been classified within the accepted meaning of the term. Personal services take up an annually expanded proportion of the labour force. The creation of a decent environment for human living has become the touchstone of housing and urban planning, with a marked emphasis on the conservation of natural resources and the deliberate development of recreation facilities. Encouragement of the arts is now commonly accepted as a legitimate object of public policy. These are surely among the "extravagances" that Dr. Adiseshiah would recommend to the rich societies. The poor societies, however, which encompass a substantial part of the world's population, will be left with the welfare problems arising from inadequate resources.

There is a vital choice to be made between the welfare services that are designed to maintain and improve the North American way of life, with its high standards of material well-being, and welfare services that are designed to redress the balance between the rich and the poor within a nation and between the rich nations

[5]Julian Huxley, *Essays of a Humanist* (New York: Harper & Row, 1964), pp. 86–7.

and the poor nations. As Professor Frankel clearly demonstrates, the choice is fundamentally a moral one. The ultimate decision may well determine the future of mankind.

There will be many who will not be satisfied to accept the values of a humanist as the ultimate test of the "proper ends of life." A very different approach is to be found in the writings of the priest-palaeontologist who found it possible to reconcile for himself the rigours of science with the mystic claims of his faith. Pierre Teilhard de Chardin wrote:

We need to remind ourselves yet again, so as to offset this truly pagan materialism and naturalism, that although the laws of biogenesis by their nature presuppose, and in fact bring about, an improvement in human living conditions, it is not *well-being* but a hunger for *more-being* which, of psychological necessity, can alone preserve the thinking earth from the *taedium vitae*. And this makes fully plain the importance of what I have already suggested, that it is upon its point (or superstructure) of spiritual concentration, and not on its basis (or infra-structure) of material arrangement, that the equilibrium of Mankind biologically depends.[6]

The contributors to the present volume pose a variety of other choices. For example, it may be said that welfare poses a choice between adopting as a goal "a standard of living," which is largely a matter of material values, or making the objective of welfare the enhancement of the quality of life, a conception in which aesthetic and moral values are inherent over and beyond material goals.

Professor Pusić poses another choice when he argues that reliance upon organization tends readily to displacement of goals, so that the "existence and growth of the organization become a goal in their own right—a goal which commands, more and more, the emotions and the motivations of people working for the organization, and dominates, by its importance and appeal, the original aims for the pursuit of which the organization was created." This can happen as easily to a government welfare service as it can be demonstrated in the persistence of private agencies whose original aims have either been achieved or become irrelevant in the changing society within which they persist.

[6]Pierre Teilhard de Chardin, *The Future of Man* trans. from the French by Norman Denny (London: Collins, 1964), p. 303. Italics in the original.

The concept of welfare is in need of redefinition. Welfare has come to take a primary place among the economic, political, and social goals of a modern technological world. In order to justify this place, men will have to make choices within an expanding range of alternatives in an increasingly complex situation. These choices must be made by individuals, by communities, and by nations. If they are to be good choices, it will be necessary not only to acquire factual knowledge, which is morally neutral, but to exercise wisdom, which requires moral judgments. The justification of the adventure in ideas which this book represents must be that it expands the area of choice by making explicit many aspects of welfare that have hitherto been implicit or ignored. In expanding the concept of welfare, the quality of wisdom should be enhanced. The future of welfare, freed from the shackles of tradition and ignorance, must depend upon the wisdom with which men exploit the new possibilities, hitherto unsuspected and unplumbed, that are uncovered by the authors of this book.

T. H. MARSHALL

Welfare in the Context of Social
Development

Welfare in the Context of Social Policy

T. H. MARSHALL

Professor Emeritus of Sociology,
University of London

Professor Marshall graduated in history at Cambridge University and was elected to a Fellowship at Trinity College, where he taught English Economic History until 1926. At the London School of Economics he was Head of the Social Science Department and Martin White Professor of Sociology. In 1956 he became Director of the Social Sciences Department of UNESCO and in 1960 returned to Cambridge and took part in establishing the teaching of Sociology for the Economics Tripos. From 1959 to 1962 he was President of the International Sociological Association. Professor Marshall's collected papers have been published in a volume entitled *Sociology at the Crossroads—and Other Essays* (American edition, *Class, Citizenship and Social Development*). His latest book *Social Policy* was published this year.

Welfare in the Context of Social Development

IT SHOULD hardly be necessary for me to remind this audience that "Commonwealth" signifies "Commonweal," and since "weal" is only another word for "welfare," it would seem to follow that welfare and wealth are the same thing. But nobody remotely connected with a school of social work, let alone a school as distinguished as the one whose fiftieth birthday we are now celebrating, would hesitate for a moment to repudiate this conclusion as both false and mischievous. For, if wealth and welfare were in fact the same, there would be little need for trained social workers and nothing much for a school of social work to study or to teach. But, although we feel quite certain we are right on this point, a little thought, aided by an excursion into past history, will soon show that the distinction between wealth and welfare is not a simple one, and that it has not always appeared as obvious as it does today.

"Welfare," wrote J. A. Hobson in 1929, "may mean anything from the most elevated conception of human character and destiny to the baths, refectories and recreation grounds that figure so prominently in what is known as 'welfare work'."[1] I mention the date of this quotation in order to forestall the indignation you might feel at this somewhat narrow view of welfare work, because that is not the point I want to make. My point is that the welfare about which I shall be talking is precariously perched in the middle of this slippery slope from the sublime to the ridiculous, being less

[1] J. A. Hobson, *Wealth and Life: A Study in Values* (London: Macmillan & Co., 1929), p. 10.

abstract and subjective than "human character and destiny" but less material and objective than "baths and refectories." If it were located at either end of this scale, there would be little difficulty in distinguishing it from wealth. But in the middle, where it is found, it has wealth as a near neighbour and companion, and the relationship between the two of them is best described as one of intermittent entanglement.

For it is obvious that welfare, in the broadest sense, is achieved largely by the consumption of goods and services that money can buy, and money is wealth. And it is also true that the welfare, or social, services have been mainly concerned, during the greater part of their history, with supplying goods and services to those too poor to buy them for themselves; welfare in this sense was a substitute for money, or wealth. Yet even in this context of the things that money can buy, wealth and welfare are not identical. The economists discovered this when they began to play with the concept of marginal utility. For, as one writer puts it, "under the impact of the marginal revolution . . . economic thought started moving away from the classical materialistic level to the modern subjective level of analysis."[2] What had to be measured, in other words, was not an absolute quantity of physical goods or services, but the satisfaction gained from them by the consumer, which varies from case to case, according to circumstances. And whereas the possession of goods or of money is wealth, the satisfaction of wants is welfare.

The author I have just quoted was talking about economic welfare which, he says, consists in the satisfaction of wants "belonging to the 'material' aspects of life, capable of being brought into relation with the 'measuring rod of money'."[3] But, you will say, economic welfare is not the only kind of welfare. For of what use is the measuring rod of money in assessing the satisfaction that a social worker can give to an aged widow, a handicapped child, or a problem family? The commodities consumed in such cases include things like sympathy, courage, hope, and even perhaps happiness, and they cannot be measured in money. Should we say, then, that

[2]Hla Myint, *Theories of Welfare Economics* (London: London School of Economics Publications, 1948), p. 125.
[3]*Ibid.*, p. 122.

welfare is a special kind of happiness? That is a plausible theory, but not a wholly satisfactory one. For, just as wealth is too objective a concept to stand for welfare, so happiness is too subjective, too unaccountable, too intimate. "The pursuit of happiness," says Galbraith, "is admirable as a social goal. But the notion of happiness lacks philosophical exactitude."[4] It is true that the Utilitarians gave as their recipe for the perfect social system "the greatest happiness of the greatest number," and Bentham himself argued that a government could pursue general happiness by legislation exactly as the individual pursues personal happiness by choosing pleasure and avoiding pain. "The business of government," he wrote, "is to promote the happiness of society by punishing and rewarding,"[5] which implies that the government knows more about the happiness of the individual than he does himself. But generally speaking happiness has been regarded as something of which each man is his own judge, something too personal and unpredictable to be the direct object of policy. And when John Stuart Mill campaigned for compulsory education and Edwin Chadwick for compulsory sanitation, they hardly needed to weigh their proposals in the delicate balance of pleasure and pain; they were simply asking for the establishment of much-needed welfare services. I conclude, then, that welfare is entangled with happiness, just as it is with wealth, but is not identical with it. It must be distinguished from both of them, but can be wholly detached from neither. Wealth may be a source of welfare, and welfare of happiness, but the causal relationships are neither necessary nor constant. We could say that wealth and happiness mark the boundaries of the territory in which welfare dwells. But I prefer a different metaphor—that they are the poles of the axis along which welfare moves. For its position in relation to them has varied during the process of social development. If we want to get a full view of its nature, we must study it in motion as well as at rest.

But before I embark on this task I want to introduce another dimension, or axis, along which welfare moves. It runs between the

[4]J. K. Galbraith, *The Affluent Society* (London: Hamish Hamilton, 1958), p. 272.

[5]E. Halévy, *The Growth of Philosophical Radicalism* (London: Faber and Gwyer Ltd., 1928), p. 27.

two poles of the individual and the society, or between an individualist and a collectivist interpretation of the concept of welfare. Ultimately, of course, welfare is an individual matter, since it is only individuals who can have wants and be conscious of their satisfaction. But the circumstances which affect the welfare of individuals very often operate in and on groups as wholes—a *family* is poverty-stricken, or a *neighbourhood* is unhealthy; a *nation* is prosperous, or a *people* is free. And if one studies the question with a view to taking action to increase welfare or to diminish "illfare" (I have not invented that word; I found it in the Oxford Dictionary), one may approach it from either angle, the individual or the collective. In both welfare economics and utilitarian philosophy the main preoccupation has been with society as a whole. For the crucial problem was how to "maximize" welfare or happiness in the community. It was appreciated that you cannot arrive at the maximum total utility, or happiness, by simply allowing complete freedom of action to everybody. The actions of an individual may have effects on others that are not visible at the time and therefore do not enter into the calculus by which individual interests are brought into balance for the common good. There are concealed "social costs," and consequences which will only be fully felt by future generations. So it is necessary to make a careful study of the working of society as a whole in order to learn how best to promote the individual welfare of each member of it.

If we look at welfare in operational terms as the object of social policy and social work, we see that social workers, both in the early philanthropic phase and in the period after what one writer calls the "psychiatric eruption,"[6] have fixed their attention on the individual and his troubles with a concentration that is sometimes quite terrifying. The Beveridge Plan, on the other hand, on which British social policy was based after the war, sought to benefit individuals by collective action. It was inspired by its author's liberalism but used methods which smacked of socialism. For Beveridge's aim was to build a firm foundation for the welfare of each by offering benefits to all—a minimum subsistence income, full employment,

---

[6]Kathleen Woodroofe, *From Charity to Social Work in England and the United States* (London: Routledge and Kegan Paul, 1962), p. 128.

family allowances, and a National Health Service. He found the causes of the wants he planned to relieve in the defects of the system, and as an efficient remedy he offered the blue-print of the Welfare State. These examples must serve for the moment to illustrate the way in which the concept of welfare can move along the individual-collectivity axis.

An Englishman living in the reign of Queen Elizabeth II who wishes to set his subject in historical perspective is naturally disposed to go back for this purpose to the age of Elizabeth I, for that is as good a period as any to choose as the beginning of modern times. And it has an even stronger claim to be regarded as marking the beginning of modern social policy. It was an age of great individual enterprise, adventure, and creative power, but even more significantly it was an age in which the national community came into its own and took the centre of the stage. It is always risky to make dogmatic statements about complex matters, but a lecture is a dull affair if the lecturer takes no risks. So I will assert, with all due respect to those who may disagree, that Elizabethan England witnessed the first expression of national patriotism, the first comprehensive national policy, and the first step in the shift of interest from the revenues of princes to the wealth of nations. The aim of the government was the prosperity of the whole, and this aim was pursued by a combination of economic and social measures; any idea that these two branches of government were distinct and separate was quite alien to the spirit of the time.

But the whole for whose prosperity government strove was not a homogeneous unit. Society was a structure of segments, in part divided horizontally into layers or classes, and in part vertically into such distinct social areas as town and country, church and laity, merchants and craftsmen. Each had its way of life, its standards of value determining its wants and their expected satisfaction. Prosperity, therefore, meant something different for each, and for some, no doubt, it hardly merited the name at all. Economic and social policy combined to maintain this system and its pattern of life by fixing both the wages of the workers and the relief of the poor, by regulating both the apprenticeship of sons of well-to-do families and the setting of pauper children to work, and by the recognition or creation of liberties and monopolies by which local communities and societies of tradesmen could direct their own affairs and protect the interests of their members. If one classifies societies in terms of laissez-faire versus planning, then Elizabethan England was a planned society, but of a conservative, not a revolutionary kind. Its innovations, which were considerable, were not designed to create a new kind of society as much as to perfect and so to preserve an old one, which was believed to reflect the innate, indigenous dispositions of the people. Nor was it totalitarian, thanks to its emphasis on social groups each of which, within the limits set by the general pattern, had its distinctive character and enjoyed a measure of autonomy.

It is fair, I think, to describe the object of the plan as being welfare, and a type of welfare that lies nearer to the happiness end of the wealth-happiness axis. For it was not conceived in terms of money and goods, but rather of the kind of life that each kind of person should be able to live. And this emphasis on persons rather than on things gave it a subjective character. I fear you may imagine that I have fallen an easy prey to romantic tales of "Merrie England," but this is not so. I am well aware that the standards of those days were not those to which we are now accustomed, and that they were not always realized in practice. It was in many ways a brutal age, and the actions of its governments were not wholly benevolent. But it was generally assumed that the poor could be happy, and not merely contented with their lot. Shakespeare was a shrewd observer of life, and most of his humbler characters seem to lead a more carefree existence than their betters. I am quite sure, for instance, that the "rude mechanicals" in a *Midsummer Night's Dream* thoroughly enjoyed rehearsing and performing their play for the Duke and his friends. But, be that as it may, it is a fact in support of which I could produce much evidence that the emphasis was on persons rather than on things, and I am prepared to stand by that.

I propose now to take a leap forward to the end of the nineteenth century, that is to say to the eve of the second wave of social policy which was marked by the introduction of social insurance and the break-up of the poor law. It was also the age of the "marginal revolution" in economic theory of which I spoke earlier. The picture we see here is a very different one. I shall not waste your time by retailing to you the familiar features of a society whose economy is based on free competition in the market and its polity on the philosophy of individualism and on rights rooted in property. I shall confine myself to pointing out those contrasts with the Elizabethan period that are relevant to my theme. First then, in place of a society divided into segments each of which has its own appropriate way of life, and consequently its own kind of welfare, we see a whole people engaged in hunting the same quarry, namely wealth, but with the peculiarity that a very large part of the field has no chance of ever getting even a sight of the game. One effect of this is that, whereas in the segmented society the focal point of social thinking is the proper standard, or norm, for each group, in the unified, open, competitive market economy the only firm standard of any practical significance is the minimum—the minimum wage and the poverty line. Above that there is no standard, in the strict sense, because each is entitled to keep what he can get, and all are pursuing a goal which perpetually recedes as prosperity increases and expectations rise. It follows that those at the bottom of the scale of wealth are described in purely negative terms, by what they lack. They are the ill-housed and ill-fed, the uneducated, unhealthy and unwashed, the unemployed and the un-skilled; I doubt very much whether the concept of "unskilled worker" existed in Elizabethan times, when it was customary to speak of every trade as an art or a mystery. Modern sociologists who study the remains of this social phenomenon today also use purely negative terms to describe it, and write about the "under-privileged" and "deprivation."

In saying this I am not judging the past by the yard-stick of the present. I am referring to conditions which were a cause of acute and growing anxiety at the time. People were well aware of these defects in the new society, but were puzzled as to how they could be eliminated without weakening the springs of enterprise and individual effort that made society work. The evidence of anxiety is universal and overwhelming. The first objects of it were the children, and every industrial country took steps to keep the youngest of them out of the factories and to protect the older ones who were allowed into them. Then there were the old, the "aged deserving poor," as they were called, but their problem had not got far beyond the stage of agonized exploration and indecisive discussion as the nineteenth century drew to its close. In 1899 the British Board of Trade presented to both Houses of Parliament a report on "Provision for Old Age" by the governments of Russia, Norway, Sweden, Denmark, Germany, Holland, Belgium, France, Italy, Austria, and Rumania.[7] But most of it was about commissions of investigation and proposals for action on which no decision had yet been reached. For, as a British politician said in 1902, "old age pensions have almost passed into the role of platitudes of political controversy . . . the things that everybody may talk about with a consciousness that nothing will be done."[8] But something, though not very much, had been done already, most notably in Germany where Bismarck had made the first experiment in national social insurance in order, as he said, by satisfying the legitimate claims of the working classes, to discourage them from pressing their illegitimate ones. And gradually, in one way or another, his example was followed.

Finally, dissatisfaction with the operation of the Poor Laws, or Public Assistance, was widespread, and it increased in intensity as the new century advanced. The movement for reform developed along two lines. First, it came to be recognized that there were certain classes of poor people who ought not to be treated as paupers, namely the children, the old, the sick, and the unemployed. When special arrangements were made to meet their needs, the first step had been taken towards the so-called "break-up of the Poor Law." Secondly, attempts were made to humanize the treatment of those who remained in the pauper category. It was, no doubt, a bold innovation when, in 1929, New York renamed its Poor Law the Public Welfare Law, and declared that the authorities should do everything necessary for those "unable to maintain themselves," in order to "restore such persons to a condition of self-support." But old ideas die hard. Edith Abbott, writing in 1940, said that "many of the old deterrent features of the poor laws are, unfortunately, still very widely accepted as necessary and

[7]"Provision for Old Age by Government Action in Certain European Countries," *Parliamentary Papers*, vol. 92 (1899).

[8]Sir Arnold Wilson and G. S. Mackay, *Old Age Pensions: An Historical and Cultural Study* (London: Oxford University Press, 1941), p. 37.

proper methods of granting public relief."[9] Things moved faster in Europe, and in Britain they were accelerated by the two reports of the famous Royal Commission of 1905–9.

I will not pursue the story further, as it is no doubt familiar to you. The points I wish to make are these. Of course the transformation of a segmented into an open society was a necessary condition of social and economic development, and of course the standard of living was in many respects higher in 1900 than in 1600. But the new society had lost the old, positive concept of welfare and had not yet found a new one that could take its place. In the case of the economically successful, welfare was assumed to flow automatically from wealth, and no problem of public welfare arose for them, except in the matter of drains. The only direct concern with individual welfare manifested itself at the bottom of the scale, around the poverty line, and the action it inspired aimed only at making life tolerable. I need hardly underline for you the contrast between this and the modern conception of welfare which aims, not at the lowest that is tolerable, but at the highest that is possible. We must not blame too much those who, more than half a century ago, thought that the relief of the poor should be enough only to keep them alive under conditions sufficiently unpleasant to deter others from giving up the struggle to maintain themselves and their families. For this attitude was all of a piece with the social system in which they lived, and they knew no other.

The situation today is very different from what it was then. Changes have taken place both in the social system and in the concept of welfare, and they have reacted on one another. I propose to discuss these under three headings which may be briefly described as the relation of welfare with wealth, with individualism, and with equality.

The twentieth century has witnessed the transformation of the wage-earning classes from a mere labour force, or instrument of production, into a body of consumers for whose custom industries compete by studying their tastes, catering for their wants, and stimulating their appetites. The money they spend in the shops is

[9]Edith Abbott, *Public Assistance: American Principles and Policies* (Chicago: University of Chicago Press, 1941), vol. I, pp. 60 and 35.

just as essential a contribution to the prosperity of industry as the work they do in the factories. This means that, in terms of the metaphor I used earlier, most of the field following the hunt get a share of the game, or, in other words, new social classes are able to join the general chase after material wealth with some hope of success. Does it follow that the inclination to identify welfare with wealth becomes even stronger than it was already? I think not.

It is often said—and I have said it myself—that the Affluent Society encourages the cruder forms of acquisitiveness. The result could be disastrous, if there were not strong counteracting forces present. And among these today is a concept of welfare which has been progressively detaching itself from a too close association with material wealth. It is not easy to be precise about the cause of this. But surely it owes much to the rising standards of health and education, and the great importance attached to them; to the increase of leisure and the possibilities open to all—or nearly all— for the enjoyment of holidays; to the gradual transformation of the physical environment of the home and the neighbourhood, and so forth. And there is much evidence to show that many people in the middle ranks of society prefer a secure, and interesting job, with a moderate income, to a precarious struggle for money and power— though whether that is always a good thing may be open to question. It is, I think, fair to say that, as affluence spreads down-wards through society, there takes shape in the minds of those who join the ranks of the comfortably-off a picture of the kind of life they want to live—a picture that is complete, concrete, and realistic, be-cause they are thinking about something that is within their reach. This is very different both from the old struggle to keep the family's head above water, and from the obsessive passion to make money and to accumulate wealth at all costs. The former is materialistic of necessity, and the latter of choice. But a sane interest in spending money in a manner that will yield the maximum enjoyment need not be materialistic at all, unless you insist on comparing it with the behaviour of the religious ascetic. The "conspicuous consumption" noted by Veblen and the purchase of status symbols observed by modern sociologists do not, I admit, have anything much to do with welfare in the true sense of the word, and they are still with us. But the "inconspicuous consumption" (if I may use the phrase) of those who spend as others do to build up their little model of the popular culture of the day is, I think, concerned with welfare and with a conception of it which has moved some way towards the happiness pole of the wealth-happiness axis. It is the modern version of what the British politician and publicist, Masterman, was referring to when he wrote in 1909 that "the new civilization of the Crowd has become possible."[10] And today we are all, more or less, members of the same crowd. What I am suggesting is that the "affluent societies" of the mid-twentieth century contain within themselves elements producing a discord that has not yet been resolved, and which, I may add, could remain unresolved for a long time without disrupting the social order. There is on the one hand the spirit of acquisitiveness, stimulated by prospects of easy money, and on the other the pursuit of civilized enjoyment, which has close affinities with welfare. They could coexist, in a rather uneasy equilibrium, almost indefinitely. But in the long run I fancy that the scales may be weighted in favour of the second, partly because I believe that, in the long run, it represents the natural reaction of the majority to a rising standard of living, and partly because it receives the powerful support of collective action in favour of common enjoyment and general welfare. And I shall have more to say about that in my second lecture.

I come now to my second point about the contemporary situation, namely the relation of welfare with individualism. It is commonly asserted that the nineteenth century was the age of laissez-faire individualism and that the twentieth—at least after the second world war—is the age of the "mass society," and the assertion, like most of its kind, contains a modicum of truth. The term "mass society" belongs more to the language of journalism than to that of science, but the social phenomena to which it refers are easily recognized. There is first the physical congestion in our urban centres and public places, and the ever-increasing proportion of the population that spends an ever-increasing proportion of its time in a crowd, fighting to preserve its individual dignity against the crushing pressure of numbers. Then there is the prevalence of the techniques of mass production, in which individuals become

[10]C. F. G. Masterman, *The Condition of England* (London: Methuen & Co., 1909), p. 133.

undifferentiated atoms in labour units engaged in limited, repetitive, impersonal tasks which are themselves only a minute part of a total process of production. And finally, and perhaps most important of all, there are the forces of mass communication, and, if we are not very careful, of mass education, which operate in the same way, at the same time, and with the same content on the minds of all those within range of their influence. They are inescapable, but they are also indispensable to modern social life. Add all these together, and you may well conclude that the civilized crowd whose birth was proclaimed by Masterman over half a century ago has failed to fulfil its early promise, and has now been ousted and replaced by the "Lonely Crowd" of David Riesman, whose members "can no more assuage their loneliness in a crowd of peers than one can assuage one's thirst by drinking sea-water."[11] The individual is lost in a host of repetitions of himself.

But here again, I think, we have an unresolved discord and an uneasy equilibrium of opposites. For, paradoxical as it may appear at first sight, there are important ways in which the mass society cultivates the individual, and they are closely associated with its concept of welfare. For welfare, as I have already said, must ultimately be an affair of the individual, even though it may be furthered by collective action. But, you may well ask, how can welfare do anything to redress the balance between the individual and the mass that was not already being done more effectively by the laissez-faire individualism of the nineteenth century? The answer is, I think, that nineteenth-century individualism was rooted in rights, but only in certain rights of which, as Tawney insisted in his analysis of "The Acquisitive Society," the rights of property were the most important. And the image of the individual as a repository of rights lacked humanity; it suggested an apparatus rather than a person. Nineteenth-century individualism, in fact, did not fully recognize, or realize, the individual. Now the twentieth century has shown that the right to welfare contains within itself the possibility of remedying this defect and filling this gap. For welfare, like peace, is indivisible. However specialized the services it offers, it must always keep in view, and pay respect to, the integrity

[11]David Riesman, *The Lonely Crowd* (New Haven: Yale University Press, 1950), p. 373.

of the whole person. And it is only this kind of individualism of the whole person that can resist the assault of the mass society against the individual personality.

Education perhaps offers the best illustration of my point. I said just now that we must take care to see that the education of the masses does not degenerate into mass education. It is clear that there are inevitable tendencies in that direction, due to the need to handle vast numbers of students with a sufficient degree of uniformity to maintain general standards and to make educational qualifications comparable. But these may be, and to a great extent are being, balanced by attempts to give each individual the education best suited to his capacities and interests, and to adopt methods of teaching and to create conditions in schools which may be expected to encourage the free development of personality. And nowhere is this more in evidence than in the junior classes of primary schools in which, not so very long ago, the children learned by rote and chanted their lessons in chorus. We find a similar situation in our modern health services in which we try hard to combine large-scale organization and hospital discipline with an imaginative concern about the physical and psychological needs of the individual. The problem was seen very clearly even before the war by the distinguished British physician, Lord Dawson of Penn, when he said that the main difficulty in establishing a National Health Service was to combine socialism in its administration with individualism in its practice.[12] And nothing is more impressive than the extent to which the rapidly expanding public welfare services have succeeded in combining administrative bureaucracy with an intensely personal view of the needs of those afflicted by physical, mental, or social disabilities. But of this, too, I shall speak further in my second lecture.

My third comment on the present situation refers to the relation of welfare with equality. It is the most difficult to elucidate and I hope I can leave the profounder study of it to subsequent speakers in this series of lectures. I shall confine myself to my theme of the unresolved discord and the uneasy equilibrium in modern societies and the part which welfare plays in adjusting the balance.

Everybody would agree that the evolution of modern society

[12]"Bill of Health," *The Economist* (March 30th, 1946), p. 483.

has been deeply influenced in various ways by egalitarian ideas and conscious efforts to put them into practice. One thinks of the granting of universal suffrage in the democratic countries; the elaborate systems designed to give equality of opportunity in education and therefore, at least at the point of entry, in careers; the organization of medical services to provide at least the essentials, and in some cases much more than that, for everybody; the building up of institutions of common enjoyment in various branches of culture; and the gradual elimination—a slow and difficult process—of slums and their replacement by flats and houses which a visitor from Mars would be able to distinguish from the homes of the "upper classes" only by their internal decor and the ratio of bathrooms to bedrooms. But in spite of this, and in spite of systems of social security which redistribute income from the richest to the poorest, in no country, whether governed by the principles of liberal democracy, socialism, or communism, is there anything approaching an equality of money incomes. And the inequality of incomes, and more particularly of earnings, is there, not because it has resisted all efforts to get rid of it, but because it is accepted in principle as a necessary and legitimate feature of the social order.

Such is the unresolved discord and uneasy equilibrium in the case of equality, and the uneasiness is conspicuously displayed in the endless series of claims for, and disputes about, increases in wages and salaries which disturb the economic life of most industrial countries today. It is clear that, although unequal incomes and differential earnings are accepted as legitimate, there is no general agreement about the principles by which the inequalities and the differences should be regulated. Both the major political parties in Britain today talk about the need for an incomes policy, but neither has yet been able to produce anything that looks like a workable plan of action.

While these economic inequalities are visible to all, and a perpetual source of irritation to some, the equalities of other kinds which might balance them are less obvious, and some of them appear, on closer examination, to be deceptive. It is true, for example, that the franchise in democratic countries follows the principle of "one man (and one woman) one vote," but although the denial of the franchise to a social group may mark it with the badge of inferiority, I doubt whether its possession by everybody does much to modify the effect of the more obvious inequalities of the social and economic system. Robert Michels, in his well-known book *Political Parties*, quotes a nineteenth-century Frenchman as saying: "When I voted, my equality tumbled into the box with my ballot; they disappeared together."[13]

Equality of opportunity in education is very difficult to establish in practice and its effect, in so far as it exists, is not to eliminate differences of educational experience, occupational ranking, and social status, but only to change the process by which they are shaped. And the more ardent egalitarians are now saying that if it is unjust that a man should get educational, occupational, and financial advantages simply because he was born rich, is it any less unjust that he should benefit in this way simply because he was born clever? In neither case can he claim any personal credit for his superiority over others.

Social security is a device for maintaining, that is to say equalizing, incomes. Critics, however, point out that more of the redistribution of income it causes is lateral, between people of roughly the same income-group, than vertical, between rich and poor. Lateral redistribution can, of course, be beneficial to all concerned by acting as a sort of collectively organized method of saving for a rainy day, but excessive concern with it may prevent the flow of income from being directed towards that section of the community whose need is the greatest. Free or subsidized services, in education or health, may appear to equalize real income, but, say the critics, the extension of such services from the working to the middle classes benefits the latter more than the former. This is a superficial view. For it is beyond question that the British National Health Service has raised the level of medical care for the working classes far above what it was before, and the benefit they have gained thereby is not diminished by the fact that the middle classes share in it.

All these things have the effect, as Tawney said as long ago as 1929, "of correcting the gravest results of economic inequality," and they have the great advantage of doing this in a way that "produces the maximum of social benefit with the minimum of economic disturbance."[14] They are flexible, progressive, and non-

[13]R. Michels, *Political Parties* (New York: Collier Books, 1962), p. 75.
[14]R. H. Tawney, *Equality* (London: George Allen and Unwin, 1931), pp. 189–90.

revolutionary. But they are not steps on the road to dead-level equality, and they do not contain within themselves any standard by which we can judge how far the equalizing process must go to satisfy the egalitarian principle implicit in every democratic society. And it is here, I think, that the modern concept of welfare can come to our aid. For equality in terms of welfare is not something that has to be defined by calculating the redistribution of income or measuring the economic value of social services. It is a qualitative, not a quantitative, concept. In the case of some philosophies, and religions also, the emphasis on quality as against quantity has been expressed in idealistic or even ascetic terms by setting human worth and worldly wealth against one another as opposites, and arguing that "if you've happiness within yourself," it does not matter how poor you are. But I have argued that welfare does not treat wealth and happiness as alternatives, but oscillates between them and partakes of the essence of both. It is not idealistic in a derogatory sense, but realistic and severely practical. It does not renounce the world, the flesh, and the devil, but only the devil; it is deeply concerned with the state of the world and the needs of the flesh, but with much more besides. It operates on the assumption that equality of persons is compatible with inequality of incomes provided the inequality is not too great. It does not require that all work should be equally rewarded, but it does insist that doctors should regard all their patients, and school teachers all their pupils, as deserving to be treated with the same care, and that all dwellings, however different in size, should be equally convertible by the families that occupy them into homes. And that is as near as I can get to a demonstration of what I mean when I speak of a qualitative equality of welfare that can co-exist with a quantitative inequality of income.

Welfare in the Context of Social Policy

IN MY FIRST LECTURE I was concerned with social change and the ideas of welfare that went with it; today I shall be speaking about social action and the forces that have inspired it.

If you want to discover the origins of social action in the field of welfare you will find them in the family and the local group. For it is perfectly true that "charity begins at home," and as it crosses the boundaries of the family it becomes your duty towards your neighbour. There is really no alternative in primitive and traditional societies where the most powerful obligations are rooted in kinship, and where social organization, except for the purpose of war and possibly of taxation, scarcely extends beyond the clan and the village. But the remarkable thing is that this conception of the role of family and neighbourhood has persisted right down into modern times. Poor Laws everywhere have been wont to insist that the family must give all the help it can to its needy member before any public assistance is dispensed, and welfare services are generally treated as an immediate local responsibility. This is not merely a matter of administrative convenience, but one of principle. For, as the British Ministry of Health said last year in a circular on the health and welfare services, "it is *right* [my italics] that the responsibility for these services should belong to local government."[1] They represent, in fact, a neighbourly duty.

But this resemblance between past and present is deceptive, for family and neighbourhood are different things today from what they once were, and they function in a quite different setting. So their

[1]Ministry of Health, *Health and Welfare: The Development of Community Care* (London: H.M.S.O., 1963), p. iii.

persistence as welfare agencies is nothing less than a triumph of creative change and the continuous adaptation of social institutions to their environment, and a major achievement of social policy. This is most notably so in the case of the family. The early family was a large, stable, and—as compared with other social groups—powerful body, and it was the principal instrument for the transmission of a culture from one generation to the next. The community trusted and looked up to it, and it had faith in itself. Its responsibilities towards its members were its own affair, and there was no outside authority whose business it was to interfere if its internal obligations were not being fulfilled. The modern family by contrast is small, comparatively weak, and discontinuous, in the sense that it dissolves and reforms as the children grow up, marry and start new families of their own. Although it still transmits important elements of the national culture, it is by no means alone in this, and much of what it does transmit it must learn and relearn, under outside tuition, as knowledge grows and practices change.

So, as organized social welfare services grew up outside the family, in the hands both of public officials and of private, charitable societies, a curious situation developed in which the relationship between the family and the community was turned upside down. For instead of the family being the prime mover and final arbiter in the matters with which welfare is concerned, it was reduced to a subordinate role. More than that, it was only to be expected that, in a progressive society, the family would often prove to be an obstacle to advance in welfare, because the parents, being traditionally-minded and less well educated than the social pioneers, would cling obstinately to out-of-date ideas about hygiene and the upbringing of the young. The norms of behaviour were now determined and promulgated by outside experts and popular leaders, and it became the official duty of public authorities and the self-appointed task of voluntary organizations to persuade, and if necessary compel, the family to conform to them—to oblige it to send its children to school, to induce it to send them to the dentist, and to visit and inspect it to make sure that it was doing all it should to live up to the standards accepted by public policy or approved by the gentry.

But while it was being impressed on the family that it was incompetent to educate its children or to treat them in sickness, and that it must send them out of the home to receive these services or pay for the experts to come into it, its other more general functions—the upkeep of the home, the care of its aged members and of its children, the maintenance of the decencies of family life—all these remained one hundred per cent its own responsibility. If it failed here, and was forced to appeal for help either in the home or in one of the institutions established for the purpose, this was judged by all around to be a shameful thing. And the help it then received was no longer given without question by relations and neighbours; it was the carefully measured, elaborately conditional help that was ground out of a machine operated by a local bureaucracy.

It may be that I have been guilty here of overstating my case, and it should be clear that what I have said applies with full force only to families in the lower layers of the social pyramid, and above all to those precariously balanced on the knife-edge between respectable independence and shameful pauperism which we call the poverty line. But I have a point which it is difficult to make briefly without some overstatement. It was necessary to social development that the range of functions of the family should be curtailed and its pre-eminence in the society reduced in this way. It was equally necessary, not merely that the functions left to it should continue to be carried out as before, but that they should grow in breadth and in depth to match the rising standards of a progressing society. The first trend stressed the limitations, in fact the weakness, of the family, and the second its strength. But the two trends were not incompatible. They were so only as long as the neighbourhood and its welfare bureaucracy did not stand by to help the family to succeed in its continuing functions, but stood aside waiting for it to fail.

Fortunately the family survived the test. It continued to do those things that it had to do, which could not safely be entrusted to any other agency, and it did them better as the prosperity of the society increased and the level of its education rose. The role of the family changed with the times, but the family did not decay. And that is why it has been possible to elevate it to its proper place in the world of welfare—not by restoring lost functions to it, but by accepting it as a full and indispensable partner with its own particular job to do in the total welfare enterprise. Today, I suggest, we recognize three types of social service—the statutory, the voluntary, and the family, which is the original and basic one. And their integration into a single, complex but unified welfare system is the outstanding achievement of the modern world in this field of endeavour.

In the case of the neighbourhood the critical point came when the major responsibility shifted from the spontaneous benevolence of neighbours to the formal machinery of local bureaucracies. It is obvious that a modern nation state, anxious that there should be some uniformity in the services offered by local communities, could not leave it entirely to undisciplined neighbourly instincts to take care of an important part of local affairs. For one's duty towards one's neighbour did not express itself at that time so much in the collective action of a social group for the benefit of its weaker members as in isolated individual exercises of the virtue of charity, often from motives which were not wholly charitable. The result was that, while some charitable enterprises, like the founding of hospitals, were of incalculable value, others were misdirected, wasteful, or just inefficient to a degree that made their supersession by bureaucracy inevitable.

Judging by the nomenclature used by some of these bureaucracies one might imagine that they intended to incorporate into their own systems the neighbourly spirit that had inspired those they superseded. The mayor who was the head of public assistance in the French Commune was styled "Representative of the Poor" and it was his business to defend their interests and to receive and administer bequests made to them by charitable neighbours.[2] And the English Poor Law of the nineteenth century was presided over locally by people called "Guardians" of the poor, a term which also suggests disinterested devotion to the welfare of those who were their "wards." But in this particular context the word soon lost its benevolent connotation, and it must be admitted that everywhere these early welfare bureaucracies won the reputation of doing their duty with a severity and a lack of generosity very different from the spirit that we expect to find in the good neighbour.

But it is only fair to remember that in these early days, and I am

[2]Emily G. Balch, *Public Assistance of the Poor in France* (Baltimore: American Economic Association, 1893), pp. 169–72.

thinking now particularly of Tudor England, poverty was associated not only with want but with disorder. The Poor Law authorities had to deal not only with the needy but also with the vagrants, or "sturdy beggars"—and they were a holy terror. The settled village poor hurt nobody, but the "rowsy, ragged rabblement of rakehells," as Thomas Harman called them, were a continual menace. "Hark! hark! the dogs do bark, the beggars are coming to town!"—and you must bolt your doors and bar your windows until they chose to leave. For in that age of neat social compartments into one of which every body should fit, the vagrant was an isolate, unattached and therefore irresponsible and uncontrolled. He threatened not merely the peace of the village but the stability of the society. One is reminded of the similar attitude, on a rather different plane, expressed by the early settlers in New England, where bachelors were taxed "for the selfish luxury of solitary living" and persons convicted of "living from under family government" were ordered "forthwith to submit themselves to it." That the isolate was disliked because he was mobile is seen from the order issued in Massachusetts that "whereas there is a loose and sinful custom of going or riding from town to town, oftimes men and women together, upon pretence of going to lectures, but it appears merely to drink and revel in ordinaries and taverns," unmarried persons who do this are to be liable to imprisonment for ten days or a fine of forty shillings.[3]

I have made this little digression in order to show you that vagrancy as well as poverty was blamed on the weakness of the family, and on its failure to keep its members in order and to get them safely married off as soon as possible. But I must not let this obscure my main point, which is the enumeration of the things that had to be done to arrive at our modern conception of a welfare service. The first, you will remember, was the restoration of the family to its proper place in welfare, by making it a full partner in a total, organized enterprise. The second was to inject the spirit of neighbourliness into the local welfare bureaucracies. I now come to the third. It is the extension of the neighbourhood until it includes the entire community.

[3]G. E. Howard, *A History of Matrimonial Institutions* (Chicago: University of Chicago Press, 1904), vol. 2, pp. 154–8.

This is, of course, the foundation on which has been built the Welfare State (or Welfare Society), and I leave it to you to decide exactly what that means and where it is to be found. Now it is obvious that a national neighbourhood cannot be based on the same principles as a local one, which is more or less a face-to-face group. In a local community charity and my duty towards my neighbour are very much the same thing. But Heaven forbid that a national neighbourhood should be based on charity. What then is the alternative? The answer, I think, can be found in the second Beveridge Report, which is much less well known than the first, and the conclusions of which Beveridge embodied in his book *Voluntary Action*. He argues that the two springs of voluntary action in the field of social welfare have been philanthropy and mutual aid. Both originated in direct personal contacts within small groups or communities. But whereas philanthropy cannot be blown up to national size and become the ruling philosophy of a democratic government, because it is typically expressed through help given by the privileged to the under-privileged, mutual aid can. For the democratic principle which informs the conduct of affairs of a local Friendly Society can also operate on a large scale. It may well be that significant changes take place when the voluntary Friendly Society or Slate Club grows into a vast national Benefit Society with around half a million members (or even in one British case three times that number).[4] But it is rather different in the case of a public system. For the principle of mutual aid in that case, when applied to a comprehensive scheme of national social insurance, is nothing else than the principle of common citizenship. And citizenship does not exist only in the context of social security; it permeates the whole life of the society and penetrates the consciousness of its members. It should therefore be strengthened, not weakened, by being universalized. So I conclude that the third task that had to be carried through as society advanced towards a modern welfare system was the organization of mutual aid on the basis of common citizenship.

And now I propose to retrace my steps in order to look a little more closely at the nature of these three tasks and to see on what resources society could draw when trying to execute them. And

[4]Lord Beveridge, *Voluntary Action* (London: George Allen and Unwin, 1948), p. 31.

I shall consider first the sense of shame that attached itself to poverty and its relief, and ask how deep were its roots in human nature. In some ways it was a curiously primitive attitude, for it was not so much the affliction itself that was shameful, as the admission that it existed, just as, according to Malinowski, the breach of a customary rule among the Trobriand Islanders often did not arouse strong feelings of indignation until people began to talk about it.[5] We seem to be dealing here with a kind of taboo which embraced the whole subject of money and was carried to the point of making it indecent for a middle-class Victorian to discuss his income even with his wife. One did not talk about such things; but the pauper was forced to, even to the Relieving Officer. This un-natural delicacy, which had such cruel results, was an aberration from the habits and attitudes of the past. There was no need in the Middle Ages to be secretive about poverty. It was a state to which the religious in their communities were bound by their vows, and it was the normal condition of most young scholars. Well-to-do Christians were genuinely worried when they remem-bered what the Founder of their religion had said about the poor, and thought about the narrow aperture through which the rich man must seek admission to the Kingdom of Heaven.

We find the same kind of taboo in the case of mental infirmity. The lunatic has often been regarded, especially if violent, as pos-sessed by the Devil, but equally often, when peaceful and trans-parently innocent, as under the special protection of God. In Eng-land, and no doubt elsewhere, village idiots in rural areas were the objects of warm neighbourly affection until in a more prim and proper age they were rounded up and confined in idiot villages, not so much for their own benefit as to put them out of sight and out of mind. So mental illness, like poverty, fell under a taboo; it became something deeply shameful, and we are still fighting against this legacy from the past.

My point here is that the bases of this attitude to social problems were of an ephemeral character, and in order to undermine it, it was not necessary to change human nature but to appeal to a dif-ferent part of it, a part which not so very long before had been on

[5]B. Malinowski, *Crime and Custom in Savage Society* (London: Kegan Paul, Trench, Trubner & Co., 1926), pp. 77–80.

top. No greater barrier can be erected between those in need of help and those in a position to give it than the barrier of shame. It inhibits the appeal, and poisons the sympathy which should inspire the reply. But its erection in this period of early industrialism was the result of a temporary emotional disturbance caused by peculiar social tensions. It was fundamentally unnatural. Or perhaps one should rather say that, while it reflected one natural reaction in man—the moral condemnation of things that are unpleasant or frightening—it violated other natural reactions which, when not inhibited, are much stronger, in particular the urge to sociability within the group. So when modern welfare policy set itself to breach the barrier of shame and replace it by the bridge of sympathy, it did not have to plant new instincts in the human psyche, but primarily to enlarge the human group. Hence the importance, to which I have already referred, of the rehabilitation of the neighbourhood and its extension, through the principle of common citizenship, to include the whole community.

The task of modern policy was further assisted by the fact that the old attitudes of charity and neighbourliness never really died. And the life-line to which they clung was hitched to Beveridge's two principles of philanthropy and mutual aid, as practised by private individuals and voluntary societies. These were without doubt the protagonists in the first part of that long and difficult period during which the western world was seeking to make of industrialism an intelligible and acceptable way of life. It is easy to belittle the contribution of private philanthropy at this time— roughly from the seventeenth to near the end of the nineteenth century—because there was so much about it that is offensive to our modern feelings, and which public policy in the twentieth century had to combat and overthrow. It is true that philanthropy produced an extraordinary mixture of good and bad, of sincerity and hypocrisy, of generosity and meanness, of devotion and indifference, but the positive achievements survived and were there to be built on later by others. I shall give you two examples of this strange mixture, one from the story of individual philanthropy, and the other from that of organized charity.

I hinted earlier that philanthropic acts were not always inspired by a philanthropic spirit. And it is true that many of those who gave or bequeathed a part of their possessions to the Church or to the poor were thinking more of the welfare of their own immortal souls than of that of the recipients of their bounty, and the Church did not hesitate to appeal to this motive. Nevertheless, mingled in with these self-regarding acts, and sometimes arising directly out of them, there was enough genuine concern for the sufferings of the poor, and enough personal devotion to their service, to keep the flame of charity alight. I shall illustrate this from the work and writings of a leading figure in the world of philanthropy in early eighteenth-century England, one Robert Nelson who was among other things a Fellow of the Royal Society. In 1715 he published a book entitled *An Address to Persons of Quality and Estate: Ways and Methods of Doing Good,* and you will find an account of its contents in Kirkman Gray's *History of English Philanthropy,* a work with which you may already be familiar. It tells us much about the charitable activities of those days and about the motives of the charitable, at least of those of "quality and estate."

Nelson explains how one can minister to the wants both of the souls and of the bodies of the needy. Under the latter heading come assistance to the widows and orphans of the clergy, setting the poor to work, helping distressed housekeepers, decayed tradesmen, and poor prisoners, and supporting hospitals. Among the desiderata, or charities needed but not yet established, are (I quote Kirkman Gray) "hospitals for incurables, for the blind, for stone, gout, rheumatism, consumption, dropsy, asthma, palsy and for found-lings; houses for young women convinced of their folly, houses for decayed gentlemen and gentlewomen, a house of hospitality for strangers, homes for converts from Popery, a school for children, called the 'Blackguard' and several other wants." We may smile at some of these ideas, but many of them are very sensible, and in advance of his time. Turning to charitable motives, we find Nelson in a dilemma. He is convinced that the poor are less severely tempted than the rich, and are therefore really blessed. But, to quote Gray again, his experience is that "religious people who are also wealthy show every disposition of remaining so." He con-cludes that the scriptures are not to be taken too literally. You need not give all that you have to the poor, but you ought to give some-thing. And you will be rewarded, for those who give to charity are investing (and here I quote Nelson himself) in "so many spiritual banks where their money is secured by the word of infallible truth, and where profit is as durable as their souls."[6]

What a strange mixture of good intentions, common sense, and hypocrisy! Here we find as frank an admission as you could want of the smug, self-regarding motives of the charitable, of whom nothing is asked but their money. And yet the purposes on which the money is to be spent take the form of personal services, the list of which does at least give the appearance—in spite of some oddities included in it—of having been drawn up on the basis of a classification of real wants. Reverting to the analysis I offered in my first lecture, I would say that the emphasis here is on persons rather than on things, on welfare rather than on wealth, and that the approach is individual rather than collective. This is still more marked in the appeal of a predecessor of Robert Nelson who wrote, forty years earlier: " 'Tis advisable that the alms-giver bestow his charity with his own hands. That he do both inquire out for the Needy, and afterwards relieve them himself. . . . Let him visit the sick and wounded poor people, and dress their wounds with his own hands if he can, or at least see them dressed."[7] Let him, in other words, model himself on the Good Samaritan, whose story, you remember, was told in answer to the question "And who is my neighbour?".

This interpretation of one's duty towards one's neighbour in terms of personal devotion and practical service to meet individual needs was, I suggest, kept alive by private philanthropy until, hesitantly in the nineteenth century and with rapidly growing insistence in the twentieth, it came to influence public policy. Examples can be found in all countries, but in my own one thinks of the work of the Quakers for the mentally ill, of John Howard and Elizabeth Fry for the prisoners, of Florence Nightingale and the nursing of the sick, of Octavia Hill and the housing of the poor, and of Lord Shaftesbury, who said with reference to his Ragged Schools, "I feel that my business lies in the gutter and I have not the least intention to get out of it."[8]

These were the cream—utterly sincere, enormously generous, and

[6]B. Kirkman Gray, *A History of English Philanthropy* (London: P. S. King & Son, 1905), pp. 84, 94–5 and 97–8.

[7]*Ibid.*, p. 85.

[8]Beveridge, *Voluntary Action*, p. 160.

personally devoted without reserve to their cause. Their influence was great and lasting, not least through their work as propagandists. For, by their untiring efforts to spread knowledge of the facts, they were able to breach the walls of ignorance, shatter complacent prejudice, and open the eyes of those who were blind only because they would not see. The result of their efforts, aided by the forces of social change, and in due course by the official reports of Royal Commissions, was the awakening of what we call the social conscience of the people.

My second subject is the organization of charity, and it is natural that I should choose as my example the Charity Organization Society founded in London in 1869. I said earlier that the defects of indiscriminate charity made necessary the establishment of local welfare bureaucracies. It also led directly to the organization of private philanthropy. It was not simply a question of founding societies to administer particular benefactions or to provide services to meet particular needs. The aim of the C.O.S., which means of its famous secretary C. S. Loch, was to co-ordinate the whole field of voluntary social work and to bring it into close co-operative relationship with the public services. In principle Loch was right, though he was too much inclined to think that co-ordination meant control. For only when charity was organized could the voluntary and public agencies interact and cross-fertilize each other and so move towards the close partnership which they have achieved today. And for this it was also necessary that the voluntary societies should move nearer to the model of bureaucracy, in the sense of being more efficient, systematic, professional, and impersonal. But it was here that the C.O.S. came to grief, by allowing the bureaucratic element to stifle the philanthropic.

It is customary today to decry the C.O.S. as a reactionary force whose main achievement was the development of what Professor Titmuss recently called "the technique of instructing the poor how patiently to manage their poverty."[9] And it is true that Loch's philosophy accepted the existing social system, with its class structure, and believed that the task of a welfare service was to help the poor to fit into it. He held that the causes of poverty and social

---

[9]*Link: Jubilee 1912–1962* (London: Department of Social Science and Administration of the London School of Economics and Political Science, 1962), p. 3.

failure must be sought in the individual, not in the social order. It is also true that cases were divided into the "deserving," which the C.O.S. could accept, and the "undeserving" which must be left to the Poor Law, and the distinction was largely a moral one.

Nevertheless these unhappy features of C.O.S. policy were in many cases the effect of a misguided application of principles which were in themselves sound. Loch believed that the first aim of charity must be to prevent destitution and the second to restore the destitute to independence. "Pauperism," he wrote, "is the social enemy of the modern State. The State wants citizens." How true! He also maintained that relief should not be given unless it could be adequate, and that no case should be taken up unless there were good prospects of carrying it through to a successful conclusion. This was possible only with those who were willing and able to make the effort to help themselves. And they, of course, were the "deserving." And it is interesting to note that after a time the entry "undeserving" disappeared from the case records of the C.O.S. and was replaced by "not likely to benefit," a phrase which at least concealed the underlying moral judgment. As regards the methods of operation, Loch stated that "charity requires a social discipline; it works through sympathy; it depends on science. . . . Its first thought is to understand." Again, how true! And it was under his guidance that the C.O.S. developed the first major social casework system in England, with all the apparatus of visits and investigations, of case papers and case conferences. And he held that in private philanthropy personal service should largely take the place of monetary relief. But these principles were applied with a harshness that offended even some of the Society's sincerest friends, and personal service all too often took the form, in Loch's own words, of "personal influence and control."[10] So it became one of the first tasks of the modern welfare movement to fight the philosophy and the practices of the C.O.S., and the society itself eventually found it necessary to break the association with its own past by changing

[10]C. S. Loch, *Charity Organization* (3rd ed.; London: Swan Sonnenschein & Co., 1905), pp. 4, 35; C. S. Loch, *How to Help Cases of Distress* (5th ed.; London: Longmans Green & Co., 1895), p. ix; C. L. Mowat, *The Charity Organisation Society, 1869–1913, its ideas and work* (London: Methuen & Co., 1961), pp. 37, 71.

its name to "Family Welfare Association." And yet I would still maintain that the organized philanthropy of which the C.O.S. was an outstanding example was, in spite of its great defects, a part of the life-line that linked the casual benevolence of pre-industrial times with the highly systematized, but at the same time humanized, welfare services of today.

Of the other strand in the life-line, mutual aid, I need say little here. It continued to go from strength to strength, from Craft Guilds to Friendly Societies, Trade Unions and Co-operatives. They all had their problems, and the failure-rate among Friendly Societies was often far too high, especially when they offered pensions in return for annual contributions. Then commercial companies grew up alongside them practising so-called Industrial Assurance, and operating for profit. They were not always very scrupulous, and many people were unable to distinguish clearly between them and the genuine mutual benefit societies. But the movement never died; on the contrary it flourished, and it eventually provided the model for national social insurance. In fact attempts to follow the model too closely, or at least to appear to do so, have often obscured the very real differences that distinguish schemes of compulsory social security from systems of voluntary mutual aid. But these are matters into which I cannot enter here, beyond stating that these differences, profound though they are, are not so fundamental as to invalidate the assertion that the principles of mutual benefit, evolved by voluntary action, have been translated into the principles of national social insurance, and that their contribution to modern social policy has thus been a decisive one.

I turn now from the broader issues of social policy to the more restricted subject of welfare services in the technical sense of the term. These have emerged from the womb of the Poor Law and have won their place in modern society by washing away the taint of shame and deterrence that clung to it. This has proved to be a long and difficult process which even now has not been completed. It involves the acceptance of two principles which are quite fundamental. The first is that there can only be one standard of welfare, which should be common to both statutory and voluntary services, and it is the standard, not of the minimum but of the optimum. This principle is revolutionary because when carried to its logical conclusion, it dismisses social class as irrelevant in the context of welfare.

In my own country one can trace its origins back for fifty years or more. We see it penetrating the fastnesses of the Poor Law in 1910 when the Guardians were told to base outdoor relief on "the normal standard of income on which a woman may reasonably be expected to bring up her family, regard being paid to the cost and general standard of living."[11] Note particularly the words "normal" and "general." A common standard cannot, of course, be an absolute one, but it is relative, not to the individual concerned, but to the level of civilization of the society; it reflects precisely the "normal" and the "general," though the implications of this were certainly not clear in 1910. We see it, too, in a different way in the maternity and child welfare services which began at about the same time. I imagine, though my experience in these matters is slight, that when you are weighing a naked baby on a pair of scales, the idea of social class does not obtrude itself unduly.

The second principle is complementary to the first, and looks at the matter from the angle of those entitled to receive the services. Here too it is a question of excluding the idea of social class, or more particularly, in view of the origin of welfare services, of poverty. The institutional care of the old and the children grew up within the Poor Law, and those who accepted it entered the category of paupers; this was true even of those treated by the Poor Law medical service. And this meant, of course, that nobody who was not poor, and extremely so, would dream of applying to these services for help. Recently I put this question to two or three people in charge of welfare services in various parts of England. "Is it true," I asked, "that poverty is now irrelevant to welfare service?" The reaction was much the same in each case—a slight pause, a reflective nod of the head, and—"Yes, I suppose so," and then quite firmly, "Yes, it is." The hesitation is natural, for the issue is not simple.

It would be absurd to deny that poverty is an important factor in most situations in which the need for welfare service arises. But

[11]Sidney and Beatrice Webb, *English Poor Law History: The Last Hundred Years*, part II (London: Longmans Green & Co., 1929), p. 732.

it is not poverty in the old sense of destitution, but rather lack of financial means to cope with a difficult situation. This does not mean that poverty must be present, and be proved to be present, before the case can be taken up. The case starts with an investigation of the need, and poverty enters only in so far as it is an element in the need. When the treatment has been decided on, then the question may be asked—how much can the client afford to pay for the service given? That is what happens today in England when children are taken into care and when old people are admitted into Homes; and it shows that the elimination of class and poverty as irrelevant, both to the standard of the service and to the delimitation of the clientele, does not necessarily imply that all public services must be provided free of charge.

Now it is perfectly true that in some of the principal welfare services—for the aged, the children, the homeless, and the problem families—the clientele is drawn chiefly from the poorer, even though not from the poorest, classes of society. But others who belong to a higher economic and social stratum can, and increasingly do, make use of them, and their proportion increases as one moves further into the range of services with a medical element—services for the blind and the deaf, or for the physically or mentally handicapped. And my two principles reach their final testing-point when we come to the general health services themselves.

This, as you know, is a point on which practice varies and controversy rages, and I have no intention of letting myself be engulfed in it. In some countries medical care is a public service which everybody must use, because there is no other. In my own country the hospitals are a public service and general practice a national service, but there are private alternatives used by a minority. But this minority is not a class; those who use the National Health Service, and who form the great bulk of the population, include people from all classes and pretty well all income groups. The service is not given as an insurance benefit, but as a right enjoyed by all citizens. It is not charity offered by the few to the many. It is a system of mutual aid operated by the citizens through parliament, local government, and a host of boards and committees on which doctors and laymen (unpaid) sit and work together. And what of the standard? Aneurin Bevan was determined, he said, to prevent the "creation of a two standard health service, one below and one above the salt,"[12] That is why he was against charging patients for treatment. And when nearly the whole population uses the service, it is obvious that this standard must be an optimum. But it cannot be a maximum; that is possible only outside the national service. It is claimed, of course, that there is no difference in essentials, but only in frills and luxuries, but no precise meaning can be attached to these phrases. It is said that nobody is prevented by class or poverty from getting the treatment that his illness demands. This is both true and untrue. No national service can give everybody the best possible treatment, because so often in medicine the sky's the limit. But it is true that these are the lines on which the service is run. What has been achieved so far is the utter rejection of the notion that it is permissible deliberately to offer, in matters of health and welfare, a second-class service for second-class people—and that is something. I regard this as an intrinsic quality of twentieth-century civilization.

That is all I can say here about the standard and the clientele. My third and last point concerns the executants—those who operate the services. I said earlier that nineteenth-century philanthropy sought for the causes of social problems in the individual, not in the social order. It sometimes found them in the individual case, that is to say in some external misfortune, and sometimes in the individual character. The social workers and the voluntary societies for which they worked, were apt to consider that most of their cases could only be completely solved by the moral re-education of the subjects. There followed, at first in Europe, a phase in which the emphasis shifted to the collectivist approach of social reform. This enabled the welfare services to operate in a much more favourable setting. They continued, of course, to devote their attention to the individual case, or individual group, but their task was no longer an impossible one and their conception of their function was radically changed. They no longer considered that the only real solution lay in moral re-education—on this everybody would agree. But one does not find quite the same unanimity about the conception of case work which should take its place.

One function of social work undoubtedly is to see that the col-

12Aneurin Bevan, *In Place of Fear* (London: William Heinemann, 1952), p. 76.

lective apparatus of social security and social services reaches its individual goals. Those in need of help must be told what help is available and shown how to get it. Social workers are expert in these matters and, as Baroness Wootton says, "in the complicated modern world with its ever more complicated system of social services, such expertise becomes more and more valuable."[13] But that is by no means all, and as soon as we pass on to look at other aspects of the scene we run into that mystic concept "adjustment." The nineteenth-century philanthropists tried to get the poor to adjust themselves to the social system, whereas the main object of social legislation in this century has been to adjust the social system to the people.

There remains however the very real problem of the adjustment of the individual to his particular circumstances. This may be a necessary condition for reaping the benefit of the welfare services that society offers him. I am thinking here of adjustment to blindness, to physical disablement, to old age, to desertion by a husband, to loss of parents and so forth. Such cases represent the very essence of welfare. They have no necessary connection with class or poverty. A personal service is offered by which the collective provisions of social administration are projected into the heart of the individual case. And the aim of the service is to maximize the possibilities for happiness that are latent in the circumstances. I use that rather clumsy phrase to indicate that, as I said in my first lecture, welfare cannot be identified with happiness, because that is too subjective a concept; and a welfare service cannot just set out to make people happy, because that would be presumptuous. But it can manipulate the situation so as to produce an improvement that can be objectively assessed, and it can change a person's reaction to the situation by concentrating on the point of impact between the individual and his environment and taking both of them into account. In this sense I agree with Professor Gordon Hamilton that "the 'case', the problem and the treatment are always to be regarded by the social worker as a psycho-social process."[14]

But, I hasten to add, all human situations are psycho-social, and

[13]Barbara Wootton, *Social Science and Social Pathology* (London: George Allen and Unwin, 1959), p. 296.

[14]Gordon Hamilton, *Theory and Practice of Social Case Work* (2nd ed.; New York: Columbia University Press, 1951), p. 3.

the question is on which half of that compound adjective you put the emphasis In the matter of welfare, I contend, the emphasis should be bang in the middle, on the hyphen. At that point of perfect balance the social worker can exercise an expertise which is not that of the psychiatrist, a systematized procedure which is not that of the bureaucrat, and a personal influence which is not that of the moral censor. The basis of her skill is the understanding distilled from the experience of a host of similar, but never quite identical, cases, accumulated by generations of her predecessors, interpreted by social science and communicated to her in the setting of as wide a knowledge of human nature and of society as can be absorbed by the average student in the course of her education and training.

You may think that I am belittling the psychological as compared with the social element in welfare. This is deliberate. For in my estimation welfare must be envisaged as an integral part of the whole apparatus that includes social security, education, public health, the medical services, factory legislation, the right to strike, and all the other rights and legitimate expectations which are attached to modern democratic citizenship. It has its special place in this complex, a place that can only be defined in social terms. And social welfare workers have their special skills, which match welfare's special requirements and are not a second-grade version of other professional qualifications. However far you stretch the scope of psychological medicine on the one hand or of social security on the other, the core of welfare remains intact. Social security deals with averages and the masses, welfare with individuals. Medicine treats individuals, but treats them as patients who are obliged by illness to interrupt or modify their normal social contacts, and welfare takes over when normal contacts can be resumed. And this, I submit, is the distinctive function of a welfare service, in the performance of which the training and experience of social workers makes them expert—to help those afflicted with disabilities or overwhelmed by circumstances to come to terms with life as it is, or as it can be made to be, while continuing to receive all the strength and support that every social being should be able to draw from membership of the family, the neighbourhood, and the community.

EUGEN PUSIĆ

The Political Community and the Future of Welfare

EUGEN PUSIĆ

Professor of Public Administration,
University of Zagreb

Professor Pusić received his Doctorate of Law from Zagreb in 1939. He was Head of the Social Welfare Department, City of Zagreb, 1945–1946, Head of the Organization and Planning Department of the Ministry of Social Welfare for the State of Croatia 1946–1951, and Assistant Secretary of the Council for Health and Social Policy 1951–1955. Since 1955 he has held his present post, also serving as Dean of the Advanced School of Public Administration 1961–1963. Professor Pusic is President of the International Conference of Social Work and a Fellow of the Institute of Social Studies at The Hague. His publications include a number of important studies of social work and public administration.

1

IF WE DO NOT FIND A WAY, and soon, to adapt politically to the decisive increase in both productivity and destructiveness, any discussion of human welfare is irrelevant. The choice we have to make is, unhappily, as simple as that. I say unhappily, because we all find it extremely difficult to face the implications of circumstances that are really and radically new.[1] Always, however, at crucial turns in history, some momentous change in the external or internal situation has had to be compensated by a decisive breakthrough in the pattern of our thinking and functioning. It looks as if the next great inventions might have to come in the political field in order to neutralize the dangerous combination of new technological development and old ways of thinking and feeling about man in society.

[1]One of the typical defence mechanisms against an unfathomable reality is "to face the situation squarely," to try to calculate the number of the dead and to imagine the next technical tasks of those still alive. It seems redundant to point out to those who write "On Thermonuclear War" and similar "hard headed" studies the many unwarranted assumptions they make in the technical field. Their main omission seems to be not to take sufficiently into account the unstabilizing social and psychological effects of a traumatic experience of that order of magnitude.
Another reaction is to project the present into a still uncertain future. So Raymond Aron: "L'économie s'efface avec la rareté. L'abondance laisserait subsister des problèmes d'organization, non des calculs économiques. De même, la guerre cesserait d'être un instrument de la politique le jour où elle entraînerait le suicide commun des belligérants. La capacité de production industrielle rend quelque actualité à l'utopie de l'abondance, la capacité destructrice des armes ranime les rêves de paix éternelle" (Paix et Guerre entre les nations [Paris: Calman-Levy, 1962], p. 30).

I

Life in society, as far as we can see through history, seems to have been determined by two basic and complementary facts: the necessity of co-operation and the inevitability of conflict.[2]

In the history of ideas the emotionally intensive experience of conflict attracted earlier and wider attention than did the equally obvious concept of co-operation. In the early religious systems conflict is already projected into the realm of the transcendental, into the never-ending struggle of good and evil. On a higher level of religious development the metaphysical representations are retroprojected[3] into society: what are the implications of this all-embracing war between light and darkness for practical human action? Sometimes conflict is given a positive value as an expression of solidarity of the faithful and a method of spreading the faith. In other instances, conflict is transferred to the intra-personal field. Man has to combat evil in himself in order to be counted on the winning side of the metaphysical battle, or for more disinterested reasons of personal spiritual improvement.

Co-operation was given more systematic thought only when the development of economic productivity made co-ordination of human effort one of its most obvious prerequisites. The growth of commerce and industry and the concomitant need for public peace and security, which alone could satisfy the requirement of "laissez faire, laissez passer," found expression in corresponding ideologies of co-operation, in theories of natural law and of social contract. The assumed primaeval, chaotic state of "bellum omnium erga omnes" gave place to a state of "prestabilized" harmony within the framework of supposedly aprioristic rules.

In the history of institutions, however, in the reality of their

[2]The complementarity of co-operation and conflict as basic principles of social life seems to be presently accepted even by the most pronounced theoreticians of a harmonious view of society. Cf., Talcott Parsons, "Die jüngsten Entwicklungen in der strukturell-funktionalen Theorie," *Kölner Zeitschrift für Soziologie und Sozialpsychologie*, no. 1, 1964, pp. 30–49. It would seem easy to make the additional step of understanding "homeostatic" processes in society as complementary to social change.

[3]The mechanisms of projection and retroprojection have been studied in detail by Ernst Topitsch, *Vom Ursprung und Ende der Metaphysik* (Wien: Springer Verlag, 1958).

social life and whatever the current ideologies of the time, people have always had to cope with the simultaneous tasks of finding the most appropriate method of co-operating with each other and the most effective means of fighting against each other. These two aims were sometimes fused into one overriding objective: to work together in order to survive in conflict.

For a long time the possibilities of co-operation were defined by the scope of the human eye and the power of the human voice, and were limited essentially to the face-to-face group. As with organic forms, however, the range of adaptability of institutional structures is not unlimited. The increased division of labour and the accelerated rate of change have put increasing strain on the face-to-face group. The ever-more detailed specialization of tasks has called for additional precision in the determination of behaviour. On the other hand, a more rapid succession of shifts in the social situation has intensified the requirements of elasticity, of a speedier response to change. These two tendencies have exerted a heavier and heavier pressure on the existing institutional structure. Reaching the end of its capacity for adaptation the primary group has developed pseudo-solutions of considerable interest. Behaviour patterns prescribed in the most minute detail, as in marriage ceremonies or in commercial transactions, are evidence of the attempt to find an answer to the problems imposed by the advance of the division of labour. What was won in precision, however, was lost in elasticity. The initially rational definition of individual tasks lost its meaning with the changing situation, but the behaviour, learned through repetition of the same situation in the group and reinforced by a battery of social and magic sanctions, persisted as formalized ceremonial conduct. It still yielded the social benefit of generating feelings of solidarity and security, but these advantages had to be measured against the growing handicaps to practical and efficient action.

A second contradiction in the crisis of the face-to-face structure was the opposition between the requirement for greater differentiation in social relationships and at the same time greater stability in human relations. It was evident that with trade, with migration, with colonization, it was practically useless to think of all people in black and white patterns. There were in-between relationships which could be quite profitable. One would trade with people not of one's own group, and at the same time establish quite friendly relationships. It would obviously be beneficial if this kind of relationship could be made more stable—if it did not have to be conducted under the always existing risk that any such relationship could immediately turn into open hostility.

This double challenge—detailed allocation of tasks and speedy adjustment to the changing environment, and greater differentiation in human relationships and greater stability in them—was beyond the structural possibilities of the face-to-face group. In order to find an answer a new institution was necessary, and in time a new institution was evolved: organization, one of the most remarkable social inventions of man. Organization is an instrument for achieving consciously chosen goals. It relates ends to the means necessary for achieving them by setting up a stable structure of relationships among people at work. It makes possible the planning of on-going activities, the devising of detailed programmes and blueprints for action. This is achieved by dividing the over-all task into smaller and simpler parts and by subdividing these parts until individual operations are defined to the last movement, where necessary. The lines traced in the course of this process constitute the network for the co-ordination of the total planned activity and its orientation towards the established goal. At the same time the whole system can be changed with an ease and speed difficult to imagine under earlier conditions. From the most general goal to the most specific element of action, everything can be subjected to scrutiny, analysed, compared and changed in the same way in which it was introduced in the first place, by explicit arrangement. Organization is a powerful new instrument for co-operation towards the satisfaction of human needs.

Human needs, however, have to be satisfied under conditions of scarcity of resources and within human society—conditions which define conflict as a situation where the needs of an individual or a group can be satisfied only at the expense of the needs of another individual or group.[4] There are several possible answers to a situa-

---

[4]Needs, and therefore conflicts, are not limited, of course, to material necessities. They range all the way to Coser's "non-realistic" conflicts generated by the need to release tensions (L. Coser, *The Functions of Social Conflict* [Glencoe, Ill.: The Free Press, 1956], p. 156).

tion of conflict: one party dominates the others and satisfies its needs without regard to anyone else's needs; one or several parties abandon their original aims and reorient their wants towards other objectives; the conflicting parties reach a compromise where everyone gets some satisfaction but nobody fully realizes his original goals.

Each of these methods, in the course of social development, evolves its corresponding set of institutions. Domination is socially stabilized through power; reorientation is expressed through the great systems of religious thought and aesthetic creation; and compromise is regulated through the institution of contract, through systems of rules and through the judicial process.

The original methods employed within this institutional framework are determined by the type of structure available for social action generally. Power is based on actual physical violence or on the immediate threat of it; religious communion is achieved through direct charismatic experience; the institutions of compromise function in face-to-face contact only.

In conflict, as well as in co-operation, the coming of organization marks an epoch. The field of action of the different institutions is decisively widened, the methods are transformed, their mutual relationships are altered. Power develops the continuity, the territorial links and the relative permanence we associate with the more modern notion of political power;[5] religious movements consolidate into organizations of churches with a considerably widened span of influence; contracts and rule systems become independent of the physical presence of the affected parties. At the same time power becomes less dependent on the immediate use of violence; religious experience loses some of its emotional pitch as charisma becomes gradually bureaucratized; and the area of compromise is widened in an increasingly rational atmosphere. In the mutual relations among the different institutional systems political power comes to occupy a central place. As power-systems become larger and more stable, the traditional systems of reorientation, such as religion, lose some of their former conflict-solving capacity and are relegated to the

[5]The characteristic of legitimacy of power, made popular through Max Weber, pertains to a different point of view: the motivation why people obey. That some of his subjects are prepared to obey a monarch in exile does not yet invest him with political power.

inner councils of the individual—if the corresponding church-organizations do not in turn develop some form of political power while institutions of compromise are integrated into the political power system and become, at least in principle, dependent on it.

II

Organizations are groups of people who in one of their social roles are bound by specific sets of rules to apply given resources in order to achieve prescribed ends by performing one of the activities into which the overall task is divided and by submitting to co-ordination for the most efficient achievement of the general goal. The simultaneous presence of the opposite tendencies in organization—division and fusion—is the principal source of its achievements and also the ultimate cause of its demise. There can be no doubt that today organization as an institution is facing a crisis. It seems that organization has completed its circle and in its turn has reached the limits of its capacity to adapt to changed circumstances. The crisis of organization is brought about by its role in human co-operation as well as by its place in human conflict.

As indicated earlier, the tension between the need for precision and the requirement of elasticity was too great for the face-to-face group. In the same way a new antithesis between the drive towards specialization and the necessity to co-ordinate is developing into a force likely to destroy the traditional structure of organization.

The process of differentiation of labour tends, within organizations, to take two different forms. One, implied in the organizational process itself, consists in the division of complex tasks into progressively more detailed and less complex action-elements. The result of this "crumbling"[6] of work is the production line, the conveyer belt, the standardized simple action prescribed to the last detail of time and motion, and fitted into larger schemes independently of the will or even the knowledge of the individual worker. The advantages of precision and of simplicity have to be paid for by a loss of meaningfulness, by the deadening effect on the relation between man and his work.

[6]According to the expression by Georges Friedmann "l'émiettement du travail" made popular through his book *Le travail en miettes: spécialisation et loisirs* (Paris: Gallimard, 1956).

The other form which the differentiation of labour takes is that of professional specialization. There are activities which cannot be usefully broken up into simpler elements. They are based on a systematic knowledge of more complex relationships among natural or social phenomena and on the learning of more intricate skills. Here the differentiation of labour proceeds through a progressive narrowing of the range of concern, a reduction of the field of interest, while the action-processes themselves within the smaller field remain intact. A cardiologist, for instance, does not perform simpler functions than a general practitioner, nor is a specialist of international law less qualified than a general lawyer.

In organizations the differentiation of labour develops both ways, up to a point. Comparatively early in the development of the division of labour the standardization of individual operations implicit in the first method—that is of breaking up an activity into simpler components—suggested the transfer of these well defined movements to machines. But in very recent times developments based on cybernetics and information theory have made possible the construction of large-scale chains of action where the standardized elements are performed without human intervention. The development of automation spells an end to the first method of differentiation of human labour in organizations by dividing the work-process. Whatever can be standardized can, in principle, be transferred to machines. This increases considerably the importance of the other method, the differentiation of labour by professional specialization.[7]

Professional specialization leaves the specialist in possession of the necessary knowledge and skill to perform complex and meaningful activities. He is much less in danger of being separated from the meaning of his work and, therefore, much more independent. He knows his work and does not need to wait for others to assign tasks to him. Still the work of the individual specialist has to be coordinated and integrated into larger contexts. An individual physician in a hospital, a social worker in an agency, a scientist in a

[7]At least in one of the aspects of their role Gouldner's ideal-types of "cosmopolitans" and "locals" are related to the difference between professional specialization and the fragmentation of the work-process. Gouldner does not seem, at least in his original formulations, to have taken into account the probable influence of automation on the relationship between his two types (cf., A. W. Gouldner, "Cosmopolitans and Locals: Toward an Analysis of Latent Social Roles," *Administrative Science Quarterly*, no. 3, 1957; no. 4, 1958).

laboratory, a teacher in a school, an administrator in an office can make their full contribution only as their work is brought into rational relationships with the work of others. The very independence of their individual activities, however, makes co-ordination both more necessary and more difficult. The classical school of administrative science early became aware that the span of control —the number of people to be co-ordinated by one superior—was in inverse proportion to the professional level of the work co-ordinated.

The methods of co-ordination practiced within the traditional structure of organization seem to be ill adapted to the task of tying together the work of professional specialists. The work of individuals is co-ordinated within an organization by a hierarchy of superiors who are responsible for the allocation of work tasks to those below them as well as for the control and necessary correction of their work performances. With the increasing complexity of organizations and of the work done by their individual members the hierarchical method of co-ordination requires more and more of everybody's time. The flow of directives down the line and of reports up the line becomes more abundant. More time is spent in meetings and other forms of face-to-face contact. More writing and reading for purposes of co-ordination have to be done at all levels. Administrative procedures become more involved, formalities more numerous as the organizational system tries to counteract the centrifugal tendencies of specialization. This increase of co-ordinating activities, however, has to find its place within the fixed time-budget at the disposal of the organization. Co-ordination can ultimately expand only at the expense of the main activity, which is the initial social reason for the existence of the system. More co-ordination means less health work, less social welfare services, less education, less research by the respective organizations. The point of diminishing returns can be clearly seen: it is the moment when the balance between co-ordination and basic activity becomes so unfavourable that organization will no longer be the socially most economical method of human co-operation.

Also, the method of co-ordination prevailing in organizations is based on the assumption that the existing inequalities among individuals as to their respective possibilities of contributing to the common goal are, on the whole, correctly expressed through the existing hierarchy. Individuals at lower levels perform simpler tasks and have, therefore, to know less than those at higher levels who instruct and control them and who should possess greater insight into the more complex interrelationships between the more elementary contributions of their inferiors. With the possibility of eliminating these simpler tasks altogether by transferring them to machines and with increasing professional specialization, this assumption no longer holds. Those members of the organization who are directly performing its basic activity, and who are therefore at the bottom of the traditional hierarchical pyramid, have really to be the most knowledgeable and skilful. What wonder that they adjust less and less easily to the traditional method of co-ordination which is based on the assumption that the higher echelons of the hierarchy are manned by people who are necessarily wiser and whose contribution is more valuable than that of their inferiors. This new situation is finally irreconcilable with the organizational relationship of subordination and super-ordination.

In its other aspect as well, its place in human conflict, organization is approaching the point of crisis. Organization implies a substantial increase in the efficiency of power. Through organization, power becomes impersonal and can exert a greater pressure on the individual who most fears what he cannot grasp and know: he tends to respond by aggressive and hostile attitudes to power-in-organization which presents the blank facade of anonymity to his hostility. Through organization, also, power gains a stability and continuity, an independence from the turnover of its personnel never before imagined. To human ambition organization offers the prize of power without necessarily requiring the Alcibiadic[8] talents of moving people, which imply at least a minimum of empathetic identification of the leader with the led. Power based on huge organizational systems develops a gravitational pull strong enough to draw into its orbit existing interests over a wide field. The rulers rule; the growing bureaucracy derives its living and its sense of personal value from its position; more and more people feel somehow protected by power, dependent on it, or simply fear change

---

[8]The reference is to the imagined conversation between Socrates and Alcibiades in B. de Jouvenel, *The Pure Theory of Politics* (Cambridge: at the Clarendon Press, 1963).

more than the status quo, having carved, by thousands of small adjustments, a nook for themselves. Organization makes power at the same time more all-pervading and more remote, more intermingled with everyone's interests and more independent of them. Techniques developed in order to control power of a different magnitude become manifestly inadequate.

The crucial new element in power based on organizational systems is not only its increase in quantity and stability, but the phenomenon of displacement of goals. Every organization develops a kind of staying power expressed in the loyalty of its members, in their readiness to find new tasks for it when the original purpose has been exhausted, in their commitment to values implicit in what the organization has set them to do. This loyalty, however, is to the organization more than to any other value. The existence and growth of the organization become a goal in their own right—a goal which commands, more and more, the emotions and the motivations of people working for the organization, and dominates, by its importance and appeal, the original aims for the pursuit of which the organization was created. As long as these aims justify the development of the organization and contribute to its prosperity they are maintained and used in order to legitimate the organization's activities. When they no longer perform this function they are discarded and other aims are put in their place. The organization is important, not the aims. The existence and growth of the organization are becoming its institutional goal, in contrast to the functional goals which its creators had in mind. This institutional goal tends, in the long run, to dominate and to displace also the individual objectives that the organization's members might have at any time and to subordinate their strivings, sociologically as well as psychologically, to the "reason of State" of the organization.

This displacement of individual goals and interests by the institutional goal of the organization increases with the size of the organization, in order to reach a practically inescapable level of intensity in the large organizational systems which are the basis of political power. The reason of State, the cause of the preservation and the aggrandizement of the power system as such—whatever the form in which this cause is rationalized—becomes the supreme law not only for members of the organization, but also for the political rulers and even for their opponents, the "loyal opposition." A situation may then arise when mere "bystanders," the ruled, people who apparently have everything to lose by the complete subordination of their interests to the State, are drawn into the magnetic field of the system and its institutional goals. The climate created by the endless echoing process of reinforcement of emotions similar to physical induction, makes it possible to impose the existential goals of the organizational system not only against the interests that the system was supposed to serve in the first place, but sometimes also against the manifest, basic interests of all the people concerned. And, most dangerous of all, the intrinsic purposes of different large power systems are by definition opposed to each other. While it is conceivably possible, with an increase of resources, to satisfy a multiplicity of material interests formerly conflicting in a situation of scarcity, rival power goals admit, logically, of no simultaneous satisfaction.[9]

To summarize the argument: no sooner did organizations come to dominate the institutional scene than they entered an epoch of crisis resulting from the conflict in their internal structure between specialized service and the growing need for co-ordination in large organizational systems. This tension became intensified by the parallel tensions between the independence of the professionals and the presumptions of the hierarchy. Moreover there was in the social role of the organization the increasing difficulty of controlling political power based on organizations, as well as the danger inherent in the opposition between the institutional goals of different power systems.

III

The present situation, where we have to look for a solution to the institutional crisis of our society, is affected in two important ways by technological development.

The one, and most pressing, new factor is the present level of destructiveness of weapons. Conflicts which would involve their

[9]"If the purpose of States were the wealth, health, intelligence or happiness of their citizens, there would be no incompatibility; but since these, singly and collectively, are thought less important than national power, the purposes of different States conflict, and cannot be furthered by amalgamation" (B. Russell, *Power—A New Social Analysis* [London: George Allen and Unwin, 1938], pp. 179–80).

use (i.e., conflicts between large political power systems) have to be avoided. The obvious solution is the establishment of a world community. Before this can be attempted, however, it will probably be necessary to relax gradually the structural base of the big concentrations of power as well as to modify their emotional and ideological superstructures. A process of deconcentration will have to be devised which does not aim at the utopian goal of pre-organizational simplicity but is able to reconcile the increasing interrelatedness of people and their activities with an expanding multiplicity of goals, orientations, and interests.

The other important technological factor is the accelerating increase in productivity. Estimates may differ as to the moment when we have reached, or shall reach, the level of productivity where it becomes possible to satisfy the basic material needs of all inhabitants of this planet. The reality of want and poverty in which the majority of the earth's population are still living today may label as impractical all discussions of this possibility. Still the fact remains that, technologically, the possibility is within our reach. The traditionally fundamental source of conflicts among people, competing claims for scarce resources, would then play a considerably reduced role.[10] The consequence would probably be a phenomenon which we are already witnessing today in its beginnings, the dispersion of interests.[11] What I mean by the dispersion of interests is that people participate in a greater number of various interest groups than before while the hierarchical ordering among their different interests becomes less clear and less well determined. Their various interests associate them with various, and only sometimes partially overlapping, interest groups, so that it is more unlikely that large numbers of people will become polarized into large classes based upon opposing interests.

Both technological factors point in the same direction and two

[10]Barring development which can be prevented by rational action, such as "the population explosion."

[11]The term "interest" is used in the meaning "situation permitting the maximization of a socially accepted value in relation to an individual or to a group of individuals." The purely subjective aspect of interest—the motivational orientation independent from the real-world situation—is called subjective interest. An interest group is a group of people who are in the same objective interest-situation. "Conflict of interests" denotes a situation where the maximization of a value for an individual or group of individuals is possible only at the expense of another individual or group.

general conclusions can be drawn immediately about the forms of institutional transformation that must necessarily take place.

The new structures will have to be, in a way, looser and more unified at the same time. They will have to give greater scope to the individual, to his creativity, to the independence of his specialized professional contribution, to the multitude of existing interests. They will have to isolate conflicts instead of reinforcing them to the highest emotional pitch. They will have to diffuse power into a network of mutual influence instead of concentrating it. Instead of facilitating goal-displacement they will have to counteract it. At the same time, these new institutional structures will have to simplify large-scale planning, to reflect the growing interrelatedness of human activity, in order to prevent an uncontrolled increase in social entropy.[12]

In the institutional system that must now be evolved, the process of the realization of interests will have to be integrated with the handling of interest conflicts. What we identify today as the service aspect and the political aspect of organizational systems will have to be understood as two sides of the same coin.[13] Assuming a growing dispersion of interests it would, perhaps, be more appropriate to speak of diverging rather than of conflicting interests.

This new social process which might tentatively be called the process of social self-management, will have to be carried by a new institutional structure. The process of social self-management will have to provide the means to integrate the activities of individuals

[12]Students of the problem at present seem to be primarily preoccupied with the loosening of organizational structures. The tenets about the span of control are turned upside down by the suggestion to increase the span in order to prevent the managers from managing too much. Cf., W. F. Whyte, "Human Relations— A Progress Report" in A. Etzioni, ed., *Complex Organizations* (New York: Holt, Rinehart & Winston, 1961), p. 111. D. Katz feels that "we must be able to tolerate the ambiguity of a loose organization with wide margins of tolerance with respect to meeting role requirements" ("Human Relationships and Organizational Behavior" in S. Malick and E. H. Van Ness, *Concepts and Issues in Administrative Behavior* [New Jersey: Prentice Hall, 1962], p. 173). Even direct contradictions and unrealistic requirements in role definition are justified as "creative disorder" and its stimulating effects pointed out (A. G. Frank, "Goal Ambiguity and Conflicting Standards: An Approach to the Study of Organizations," *Human Organization*, vol. 17, no. 4).

[13]Here as well, usually that side of the picture is pointed out which is new. Conflict is seen as the essence of the functioning of complex organizations (cf. M. Dalton, *Men Who Manage—Fusions of Feeling and Theory in Administration* [New York-London: J. Wiley-Chapman & Hall, 1959]) and a constructive role in organizational change ascribed to it (cf., L. Coser, *op. cit*, p. 154)

aimed at the realization of socially accepted interests under conditions of diverging individual interest positions, with the maximum social efficiency compatible with respect for the autonomy of the individual contribution. Whether we shall call the institutional structure designed for this process an "organization" or invent another name for it is a matter of personal preference. But what points can be indicated to sketch, at least in outline, the emerging structure?

If the nature of the process is to be reflected in the structure, then the institutions of social self-management will have to be constructed around opposite focal points. The first pair of these points might be the individual and the work team. The important difference from organization as we know it today is a shift in accent. The starting point in organizational structuring is the overall objective. This is divided and subdivided until each individual can be assigned his function, as it were from above; and in the course of action everything is again oriented to and measured by the general goal. Organization by its very structure pushes its members into purely instrumental roles.

The new structure starts from the individual specialist who is supposed to know his function by diagnosing given situations in the light of his knowledge and applying his skill to them without any assignment from outside. This basic element of the individual contribution is then integrated into progressively wider patterns, the basic unit of integration being the work team. The work team does not detract in any way from the professional autonomy of each of its members, but it gives to each individual activity its social meaning. In tackling the situation of a family in trouble, for instance, or planning the rehabilitation of a decaying neighbourhood, the work team will be composed of social workers, sociologists, psychologists, psychiatrists, public health specialists, lawyers, town planners, architects, and possibly others. The contribution of each is independent because his very profession is independent, and it cannot be overruled except by technical argument on its own professional ground.[14] At the same time, the socially indicated objective—to help

[14]On the other hand, the dispersion of interests counteracts the possible tendency towards narrow-mindedness and one-sidedness inherent in an increasingly detailed professional specialization.

the family, to rehabilitate the neighbourhood—can be reached only by integrated action. There are situations where there can be no action at all without a team. Surgical operations or the acting of a play are obvious illustrations. The integration of the individual professional specialist into the team has to be based on his own free acceptance and has to respect the conditions imposed by his expertise. The co-ordination by hierarchical decree or by the order of a superior is unacceptable on sound logical grounds as well as for psychological reasons. It is meaningless to give anybody the responsibility of giving orders to specialists outside his own field. Within the same field, things have to be decided by technical argument on the basis of the actual accountability for the result.

We can already point to examples of this process taken from fields where professional specialization already prevails. In order to make this situation general the process of transferring standardized, routine operations in factory and office from people to machines will have to progress much beyond the point reached at present. Only when the professional specialist becomes the prevailing type of worker, and the menial worker performing simple repetitive operations the exception, can the rigid normative structure of most of our organizational systems be replaced by the freer atmosphere of the work team. But even when the dominance of the norm is succeeded by the "hypothetical imperative" of the technical rule, there will be considerable areas left for normative regulation.

In the field of human relations especially, the internalization of the norms of professional ethics and the development of other appropriate attitudes will be another prerequisite for the functioning of the individual in the work group. The successful integration then promises to be, among other things, a better solution of the problem of the opposite drives towards new experience and towards security than anything that is possible under present circumstances. In the freedom of their professional work, people ought to find a better outlet for their tendencies towards achievement than in the discipline of the organization, while the equality of the working group might be more favourable to security than the competition for hierarchical advancement.

The work group, however, is only the basic unit of a much wider process of integration. With ascending levels two complexes of problems are likely to grow more intricate: the heterogeneous character of the work and the divergence of interests. With the multiplication of the number of work teams in a system an increase in the variety of functions is to be expected. New auxiliary and secondary functions become necessary simply because of the expansion of the network. Traditionally, these secondary and auxiliary functions are the background of the co-ordinating activity of the hierarchy in organizations. In the new structures they will have to become the task of specific work teams who will service, on a basis of equality, a number of other professional teams. For example, no consequences as to the subordination or superordination of the different individuals or groups would necessarily follow from the fact that a team is engaged in testing or examining personnel for other teams, or that it is constructing and implementing a system of salaries, or keeping a number of accounts. Even today there is no reason why an executive officer of a university or an administrator of a hospital should be hierarchically superior or inferior to the different functional specialists working in the institution. By their very function the work teams performing secondary auxiliary functions for other teams will come to represent for them a sort of contact point, a platform for wider integration on a basis of service and not of hierarchical command.

Still, decisions will have to be taken, decisions on higher levels of integration affecting a substantial number of individuals and work teams and involving, to a greater or lesser degree, their diverging interests. The logic of the system requires that the interested individuals be associated, in one way or another, with decisions affecting their interests. The functional contact points between the work teams will have to be supplemented by a system of collective bodies with changing membership and very elastic rules of procedures which will have to be convened at various levels whenever a decision about indeterminate alternatives involving interests—i.e., not a purely technical decision—has to be taken. The membership in each instance will depend on the content of the decision, giving voice or fair representation to the individuals or the work teams whose interests are touched. The functioning of a hospital board or of a faculty meeting are rudimentary examples of what these interest-decision-making bodies might be. The general application of this method will require, besides much greater elasticity in composition and procedure, the invention of a process of selection by which the handling of most divergencies of interests will be kept as near their source as possible and only those will be filtered to higher levels of integration where this more costly alternative might be worthwhile from a social point of view.

The relationship between the work groups serving as contact points for other teams and the collective bodies responsible for interest decisions should be purely functional, i.e., exist when necessary, as long as necessary, and to the extent required in a specific case, instead of the actual permanent ties of organization. This also applies to the relations between each of the two structural elements and the individuals and teams involved in their activities. All these relations have to be seen as much more fluid than the present organizational rigidities.

This leads to the third pair of problems posed by the new institutional structure: what about the interests of people affected by the activities of the professional teams, as users or consumers, and not as members of other work teams? And how is the looseness of the relationships among work teams, contact points, and decision-making bodies to be reconciled with the requirement of a more dependable prediction of human behaviour in social situations?

The obvious answer to the first question is to include the representatives of the consumers in the decision-making bodies. As consumers they are vitally interested in the "product" of the work teams concerned, in the quality of their work, but not primarily interested in the personal or institutional goals of the teams and their members. The consumers, then, are theoretically in an ideal position to voice constructive criticism of the professionals in the teams. They are clearly well-intentioned with regard to the function and able to see and to point out quickly dysfunctions. At the same time their presence could function as a diluting and sedative agent on the intensity of conflict brought before the collective bodies by the interested members of the work teams. Finally they would act as an additional factor of integration counteracting possible technocratic tendencies and clannishness on the part of the professionals.

On the other hand, the participation of the consumers in the decision-making bodies, besides involving a number of puzzling issues of recruitment and representation, might run counter to the tendency towards the differentiation of work and the dispersion of interests. If brought to its logical conclusion, the principle of representation of consumers would involve every individual in all the activities from which he derives a benefit, directly or indirectly. That is manifestly impossible and irreconcilable with present levels of technological development. The basic interest of each individual is that the multitude of services and activities necessary for the satisfaction of his needs should function normally and satisfactorily without his intervention. That means that consumer representation can be only an auxiliary or temporary device, and that the basic mechanism of integration has to be found elsewhere.

My first question was how to ensure the participation of consumers in the decision-making process. In the light of my analysis, this question now converges upon my second question: how to combine a minimum of intervention with a maximum of predictability of behaviour? The conditions for the creation of some kind of automatic regulation of behaviour in society have been considered before by utopian and by more practical thinkers. The efforts to set up "steering situations," to discover "laws of the situation"[15] are not without precedent. The imposition of negative sanctions, requiring a power relationship, can be dispensed with where the infraction of rules is followed by the loss of benefits independently from any sanctioning activity. The rules of exogamy (marrying outside one's own group), for instance, were probably most effectively "enforced" by the prospect of the offender's going without dowry and missing the opportunity to establish friendly relations with another clan. The market economy, as compared with a slave-holder or a feudal economy, has a "built-in" system of sanctions, and demands the intervention of power, in principle, only in order to guarantee the rules of the game. The public service systems, such as social security, health, education, and others, can impose a rather elaborate and sometimes vexing system of rules on their consumers simply by the threat of withholding their services or benefits. There are, therefore, no essential difficulties in establishing such services organizationally outside the system of governmental administration, which is actually done, particularly for social

[15]The expression "steering situation" is derived from the terminology of cybernetics; the term "law of the situation" belongs to Mary Parker Follett (cf., H. C. Metcalf and L. Urwick, *Dynamic Administration, The Collected Papers of Mary Parker Follett* [New York: Harper, 1942]).

security, in a number of countries. Here again the intervention of power becomes necessary the moment when consumers do not want to "consume"—e.g., in order to enforce school attendance—or when the service, instead of giving, is asking for something—e.g., collecting fees or premiums. The relative number of public services of that type seems to be on the increase. Manifest danger from disobeying regulations, danger for the transgressor stemming from the situation created by disobedience, obviates enforcement in a majority of cases. It is well known, for instance, how difficult it is to enforce traffic regulation below a given level of density of traffic, while beyond that level people will tend to conform to the commands given by automatic traffic lights.[16]

Even the idea of "creative conflict" was institutionally anticipated in practical attempts at large-scale regulation, as in the mechanism of the separation of powers. In order to avoid the overriding social influence that a large system of political power necessarily has, the attempt was made to partition power. Its various attributes were vested in different carriers—legislative assemblies, courts, executives—at least in part independent of each other. Conflicts among them were not only anticipated but regarded as the main method by which they might check each other and achieve a balance of power diminishing, to an extent, their cumulative influence in the social universe.

The relationship between interest decisions and technical decisions is basically affected by the introduction of planning. The logic of planning calls for such long chains of interconnected decisions that interests can be expressed only on the most general levels and at crucial points. All other decisions are determined by previous choices to such an extent that their technical determining factors can be comparatively little affected by interests. Besides, the network of possible consequences grows so complex that it becomes increasingly difficult for the persons involved to foresee the consequences of alternative modes of behaviour. Planning, in a way, transfers the solving of interest conflicts to an earlier point in time

[16]On situations of this kind B. de Jouvenel bases his "law of conservative exclusion" and his argument for the social usefulness of power. It seems, however, that these are precisely the examples where people will have the least difficulty of finding ways to "eliminate conflicting signals" without the intervention of power (cf., B. de Jouvenel, *op. cit.*, p. 111).

before they have had the opportunity to reach dangerous levels of intensity.

With the dispersion of interests the old calculus of lost opportunities, used at one time to discredit the psychological credibility of the *homo œconomicus,* could reappear in a possibly more realistic form. More and more interest conflicts may become intra-personal instead of inter-personal. The individual deciding to pursue one of his many interests through the collective bodies for the regulation of interest-conflicts will have to balance very carefully the maximum benefit obtainable from this course of action against the loss of opportunity to follow at the same time a multitude of other interests. This appraisal might contribute significantly to the limitation of conflicts introduced into the solving-mechanisms and burdening the collective decision-making bodies.[17] On the other hand, this internalization of conflict does not mean necessarily an intensification of internal conflict in the individual. Different interests which are in conflict simply by having different subjects might well find, in one individual, an ordered scale of individual preference assigning to each of them rank and precedence.

Around the three levels of constructive points already identified, the new structures will have to be built according to general principles somewhat like the following. The starting point would have to be, not the common task, which is then subdivided into more elementary action elements, but the other way around—the expertise of the individual specialist. For example, if we plan to dig a ditch with a number of people employed, we will normally keep in mind the totality of the task—where we want the ditch to go, how deep it is to be, etc.—and assign to each of the men a task according to this common plan. It is unnecessary that each of the men should know what we are trying to do, why we are digging a ditch, how long and how deep it finally is going to be; everybody knows exactly what he has to do, and that is enough. But if we take

[17]It is interesting that in a socialist economic system as well deliberate planning seems to be supplemented by processes independent from active intervention. Nemčinov defines planning as the "harmonious co-ordination of the economic principle of conscious control of social production—in accordance with the known objective laws of economic development—with the cybernetic principle of the automatic, autoregulatory and autoorganizing flow of the economic process" (V. S. Nemčinov, *Ekonomiko-matematičeskije metodi i modeli* [Moskva: Izdatelstvo socialno-ekonomičeskoj literaturi, 1962], p. 52).

a surgical team at a surgical operation, this method does not hold. We do not have an idea of a total operation which is then to be divided into action tasks. On the contrary, each of the specialists in the surgical operation has to have his own judgment and to behave according to his own judgment, and the whole undertaking can function only if nobody has to tell each specialist what to do, only on condition that each member of the team, through his expertise and through analysing the situation before him on the operating table, knows exactly what to do.

The second characteristic change in the new situation would be the unity between administrative and political processes, in the widest sense of the term. This is a rather far-reaching change if one thinks of the implications. For example, if a faculty of a school in the university today has a meeting to decide on the curriculum, here it is very difficult to separate administration from policy-making. The people who are to decide on the curriculum will also implement it, which is usually considered administration. Their experience from their past implementation will influence their own policy decisions. Institutions like faculties, hospitals, research institutions, etc. are already foreshadowing the future general types of co-operative action.

So far, I have identified a number of changing patterns of human behaviour in the institutional situation. I have suggested that we must recognize and put to constructive use a number of pairs of contrasting and potentially conflicting roles. First, the autonomy of the individual in his work as contrasted with the equality of members in the work team. Second, the parallel functioning of professionals and administrators without hierarchical relationships as contrasted with collective bodies for the regulation of conflicts. Third, the representation in the decision-making process of all the interests at risk as contrasted with attempts at the development of self-regulation and self-regulating situations. All of these phenomena are embodied in a number of institutional examples that exist today. The critical task for the future seems to me, however, to be to investigate their mutual interconnections, to trace these interrelationships as they merge into a balanced system of social relations, and, in particular, to examine their implications for human well-being.

2

IN THE POLITICAL COMMUNITY the notion of welfare has come to play an increasingly important role. By itself the notion of welfare is an "empty" concept. Its content is determined by contingencies of place and time, some of which can be classified along certain lines of development:

(a) *The type of need.* Welfare (or well-being) in the most general sense is a state where certain needs are satisfied. The needs whose satisfaction is considered, however, are not always the same. Material needs expand with the possibility of their fulfilment from the minimum necessary to physical survival[1] to more and more elaborate levels of material comfort thought indispensable for welfare. With other types of needs it is less easy to establish a clear-cut line of development. But variety there certainly is. Emotional needs, for instance, seem to be more constant in time, less subject to expansion, than material needs, but their expression as well as the means of their satisfaction changes with the prevailing culture and the concrete institutional structures. Aesthetic values and standards change even while the aesthetic feeling itself remains relatively constant. Political needs of active participation in community affairs, of freedom, of equality of condition change in inclusiveness, in interpretation, in institutional expression. Spiritual and religious needs as well as the impulse towards philosophical speculation or ideological commitment seem to go through periods of greater and lesser intensity and generality. The basically opposite tendencies towards new experience, creative achievement, towards activity on

[1]Even "physical minimum" needs have been found in many instances to be culturally determined.

the one hand and towards security, the preservation of acquired positions and relationships on the other, have demonstrated practically unlimited variability. The content of welfare consists of an ever-changing level of satisfaction of psychological and material needs.

(*b*) *The subjects of welfare.* The number of persons for whose welfare other people feel concern and responsibility is, on the whole, expanding: from the family, the clan, the village, the tribe, towards the community, the nation, the world. Working through the mutual interaction of economic factors and moral attitudes[2] this expansion of responsibility is the source of a most significant change in the meaning of welfare. At a certain level of general acceptance welfare emerges into the political sphere and is institutionalized in two main forms.

In the first of these forms welfare may be defined as an overall goal of the political community consisting in the optimal satisfaction of interests which the members of the community have in common. "Interest" is used here in the objective sense: a situation maximizing, for an individual or a group of individuals, a socially accepted value. Very large numbers of people, in principle even all members of a community, can be in the same situation relative to a value and can, therefore, share the same objective interest. The functioning of a given economic system, for instance, might imply certain risks common to all. To share these risks, to put the help given to individuals in cases of malfunctioning of the system on the stable basis of a guaranteed right, to alleviate for the individual the paralyzing insecurity created by the risk itself—this means to satisfy an interest which all have in common, even those who would rather be left to their own devices. To satisfy common interests by common action

[2]The growing inclusiveness of the feeling for the welfare of others is not a linear, constant, and uninterrupted movement. However, without assuming its expansion in the long run it would be difficult to explain a considerable part of social development.

In a generalized attempt, on the other hand, to interpret moral values in terms of expanding and contracting circles no clear one-way trend can be discerned: "It is more illuminating to think of differences among societies in moral values as consisting of differences in the areas within which certain types of behavior are commanded or forbidden, and to think of changes in a society's moral values as consisting of expansion or contraction of such areas" (Everett E. Hagen, *On the Theory of Social Change—How Economic Growth Begins* [Homewood, Ill.: The Dorsey Press, 1962], p. 116).

requires both a growth in capacity and an increase in understanding —the productive and organizational capacity to provide for the needs of the many and the understanding that these common concerns are more important than the isolated splendour of the few.

In its other dimension, welfare might be defined as a systematic activity meant to provide for the needs of those who cannot provide for themselves by methods considered normal in a community, such as the production of goods and services for consumption in the family, or by work for which the person receives remuneration.[3]

Earthquakes and floods, the breakdown of families, or the breaking of fundamental social norms, are, hopefully, not the rule in a community. Though relatively infrequent, they do happen, however, at all times and in all systems. They as well are becoming our common responsibility. In time, these two political meanings of welfare may meet and intersect at many points, as the first becomes more concretely defined and the second expands in objectives and methods.

Institutionalized social welfare activity for the relief of special needs is chronologically older than the political ideal of welfare for all. It has grown more inclusive through the influence of several factors:

The degree of deprivation an individual must suffer in order that the social welfare mechanism is set in motion becomes less extreme, with greater economic possibilities and higher standards of a "decent minimum" prevailing in the community.

The typical form of intervention by the social welfare institutions of society moves from repression of negatively regarded "social problem" behaviour, through attempts at regulation, outright assistance in different forms, efforts towards individual rehabilitation and restoration to "normalcy," towards systems of preventive measures.

The standards for the social evaluation of problem situations and ethical attitudes towards them vary from disapproval through compassion and various forms of social solidarity to rational detachment and the notion of individual rights to social benefits.

---

[3]The term "welfare" or "well-being" is used for the first meaning and the term "social welfare" for the second. Their mutual convergence in development, however, does not help to maintain a clear terminological distinction.

The possibilities of social welfare activity are part of the general capacities for action existing in a community at a given moment, and depend on the stage of development from face-to-face groups to large organizational systems.

The methods of coping with social problem situations include giving information intended to facilitate the orientation of the individual to social reality, assigning income and providing services, extending psychological support calculated to counteract different types of stress, regulating certain "problem prone" social relationships, as well as activities necessitated by the existence and the functioning of the social welfare institutions themselves.

The professional character of social welfare activity varies from conditions where a general awareness of the existence of social problems is considered sufficient in order to participate actively in the performance of social welfare functions, through the differentiation of a body of knowledge and skills necessary to cope with them, to full professional status for the social welfare practitioners. Where specific knowledge and skills are required for the practice of social welfare they may be seen either as incidental to some other pro fessional profile—doctor, nurse, teacher, etc.—or they are acknowledged as constituting a profession in their own right.

The type of institution carrying the largest share of social welfare activity includes the family, the local community, the State and its administration, inter-local non-governmental organizations, and networks of self-governing social institutions. Social welfare activity can be the only or the principal concern of an institution or it might be secondary to another main activity which the institution is performing.

A great number of concrete social welfare systems can and do result from the interplay of the various variables (economic possibilities, methods, required skills, institutions, etc.).

On the other hand, the ideal or goal of general welfare has become politically influential only recently. It is moving from a high plane of abstraction towards operational reality in the affairs of society. In this movement several forces coincide. Increasing productivity contributes directly to higher living standards and a better satisfaction of needs by the "normal" activity of the individual.

Emerging possibilities to influence general economic conditions through rational planning and regulation tend to reduce the dysfunctional consequences of economic processes. The expansion of public services and the development of new forms of service, specially prominent in urban communities, contribute to the differentiation as well as to the satisfaction of needs. Political democratization transforms measures for the general welfare more and more into political objectives. Practical international collaboration in problems of development the world over has a very strong welfare aspect. As this activity emerges from token proportions and receives more weight in human affairs, the common aspects of welfare transcend national boundaries.

In measures like the establishment of social insurance and general social security systems it is already difficult to distinguish between the two concepts of welfare. These measures are aimed at individuals who cannot provide for their needs themselves in the traditionally normal way, but they are applied under conditions through which practically all individuals in the population pass at some time in their lives—childhood, old age, sickness—and they are aimed at risks to which a great number are exposed, such as accidents or disabilities. Here social welfare measures lose their subsidiary character and become normal methods to provide for normal and general needs.

The future of welfare in its new interpretation, general and concrete at the same time, is determined by the basic political alternatives and transformations in the world today.

With the attainment of a level of material productivity that brings within reach the possibility of meeting the material needs of all people, social welfare becomes the normal process of political and social responsibility for achieving what has been described as a "positive state of well being." The characteristics of this state are to be found in the full development of individual capabilities, the establishment and maintenance of satisfying human relationships, constructive participation in the life of the community, creative work and recreation, and in the constant re-establishment of the dynamic equilibrium between the drives towards new experience and towards security.

Activities cease to be economic in the sense that the performance by the individual of externally determined work is a condition for obtaining the material necessities of life. At the same time, social welfare is no longer subsidiary in the sense of assisting those who cannot provide for themselves. The juxtaposition of "productive" and "non-productive" activity is gradually losing its traditional significance.

In the affluent society, however, large concentrations of power-in-organization have become a present and grave danger to the very survival of humanity. The answer to that danger can only be a consciously planned process of social deconcentration throughout the institutional structure, a process corresponding to a growing dispersion of interests. New methods have to be evolved for the systematic satisfaction of a growing variety of human needs and the simultaneous handling of diverging interests. These processes and methods have a clear bearing on the concept of welfare.

The question is, what is the role of social welfare going to be in this new pattern? Is it any longer to be considered as a specific activity at all, or is it simply the sum of a great number of specialized professional performances, of attitudes and institutions, the most general aim and result of human interaction?

The attempt at an answer to this fundamental question has to proceed from the fact of non-uniformity of development. Development proceeds at various speeds in different places, reaches different stages at different moments, its thousands of elements fall into thousands of patterns resulting from the chances of history. What welfare is going to be and to mean to people and societies in all possible cases cannot be determined beforehand. Again only the most general variables of possible development can be investigated.

Even if the marginal character of social welfare is in the process of being replaced by a general political notion of welfare, marginal individual cases and marginal situations of groups are not likely to disappear at the same time. A society that did not produce stresses on its individual members would have to be a society completely without structure, which is a contradiction. In extreme cases existing structural stresses, whatever their nature, are likely to produce problem situations. By this I mean to describe those situations where the normal functioning of the social system does not lead to the expected and socially acceptable results.

With increasing productivity and changing institutional patterns the statistical frequency of different types of problems may change, but the fact of marginal situations will continue. Deviations and shortcomings from higher standards of need satisfaction might even become a much more general condition than the deficiencies relative to the physical minimum standards in epochs of scarcity. So that marginal welfare problems might really increase with a rise in expectations.

The activities involved in coping with these problems will retain the subsidiary character conventionally associated with social welfare. But at the same time they are likely to become more highly differentiated, and less the concern of just one type of specialist. It may very well be possible that the professional activity of social work will become further specialized and subdivided among a number of more specific activities based on knowledge and skill derived from the social and behavioural sciences. The present increasing subdivisions and special fields within the profession of social work, as well as the emergence of special types of applied sociologists, psychologists, psychiatrists, criminologists and penologists, urban planners, rehabilitation specialists, and many other professional varieties indicate the general trend.

Social change might be considered the one most general source of stress causing not only marginal but also universal problems. Whatever the future is going to be, change will be one of its outstanding features—change, for a time at least, with a tendency towards acceleration in the pace of change.

Forms of change and the resulting stresses depend on the stage of development of a given community. Modernization of work techniques, new materials, new sources of power, reorganization of institutional arrangements, changing occupational patterns, different location of economic and social activities, general movements and migration of people, developing population pressures, the transformation of family and community life, changing interest positions —all these general features of change have always been present. They influence the current social scene, and there is no reason to believe they will cease to be important in the future.

Change increases insecurity as old institutions are abandoned, as people lose status derived either from knowledge and technological skills that are now superseded or from traditional positions that have crumbled, as people move to unaccustomed places and occupations. As social controls break down, new situations tax to the limit, and beyond it, the capabilities of individual adaptation. People develop resistances against the forces of change and spend frustrating lives in hopeless battles against them. Whole groups are left in marginal positions, geographically and otherwise, and become a constant source of difficulties for themselves and for society.

To the familiar pattern new factors of the same kind are likely to be added: further transformation of the occupational structure through specialization, obliteration of the difference between manual and intellectual work in the wake of automation, disappearance of the contrast between urban and rural settings, dispersion of interests, deconcentration of organizational systems, and the gradual abandoning of the principle of hierarchy. All these are likely to produce modifications in human relations, roles, and status deeper than anything hitherto experienced; the corresponding stresses will necessarily be more tense and more powerful. It would be unrealistic to assume for the future that changes, however beneficient their expected functions, will occur without any dysfunctions, without their unavoidable dark sides. These dysfunctions, besides increasing the margin of problem cases, produce stresses falling generally on a great number of people and are therefore pertinent to the new generalized concept of welfare. These developments will probably result, among other things, in an even greater interfusion of social welfare with mental health thinking than exists today and has manifest general implications for the health services.

Welfare activities of whatever kind during a time of accelerated change will have to be much more versatile and adaptable than either social welfare or general welfare measures are today.[4] Neither

---

[4]Social policy will have to live up to the ideal of being "a policy which aims at a continual reform of society in order to eliminate weaknesses of individuals or groups in that society" (J. A. Ponsioen, "General Theory of Social Welfare Policy" in Ponsioen *et al.*, *Social Welfare Policy—Contributions to Theory* ['s-Gravenhage: Mouton & Co., 1962], p. 18). Social work as well has to fit into this framework, even if it stresses traditional values. It "must be an integral part of the national social policy, aiming at arousing the nation's consciousness of its situation, at the readiness of the groups to accept a re-classification, at the acceptance of new patterns for traditional values, or of new values in the traditional hierarchy" (Ponsioen, *Social Welfare Policy—Contributions to Theory*, p. 34).

a dogmatically held ideology of general welfare nor an academically hardened body of social work theories, rules, and precepts is likely to provide an answer to the quickly changing patterns of problems or to make readily available the potential resources to cope with them. Programmes will have to be planned with a much shorter range of preparation, as well as a reduced period of social usefulness.

They will have to have greater adaptability as to place, since social development in different places on this earth will proceed in different ways, at different speeds, by different methods. And as responsibility increases internationally, it will be a very complex task to devise appropriate methods to deal with social problem situations and social regulating situations at different levels and in different varieties of development.

At the same time with accelerating social change, social programmes will have to be more adaptable in time—we will have to reckon with a shorter period of social usefulness for any single programme. Take, for example, community development. Even today we are often faced with the problem that where it has been initiated and has been a positive help in a given social situation, people press on with it—perhaps because certain structures have been built and certain vested interests created—even in situations where different structures, a stable system of local government for example, are needed. And often where we have a stable system of local government, we persist in it and become quite emotional in pointing out that it is the only democratic and only possible system, when already the development of metropolitan government, for example, would really call for completely different structures—for functional, vertical structures which are not compatible with the traditional structure of local government. We will have to adjust to the idea that all programmes which we invent have a certain limited span of social usefulness, and when this span is spent we should invent something new to meet new requirements.

This has important consequences for social work education, to mention only one implication. It will be less and less possible to give people a full kit for their practical professional performance during their whole professional careers. Much more stress will probably have to be laid on general improvements of personal development possibilities, general basic training in basic sciences, and leave all the rest to in-service training and development through practice.

Non-uniformity of development means inequality of levels of living and of chances of improvement. Moreover, increased expectations, besides causing a number of practical difficulties, also intensify the resentment caused by these inequalities. Sometimes new disparities—geographical, occupational, organizational, and others—compound old prejudices. Inequality and its consequences are probably the deepest and most important sources of tension and conflict in the world today, within individual countries as well as between them. Inequality sometimes results in different standards of value being applied to identical situations. Living conditions in a country, for instance, may be accepted by a part of the population as normal conditions of life, while they are regarded by others, applying values developed elsewhere, as unacceptable. Too great a discrepancy between goals and possibilities, between hopes and reality, instead of stimulating effort can lead to discouragement.

The new structures for co-operation, the collaboration of specialized individuals in working teams, co-ordinated flexibly and autonomously through specialized contact points and through decision-making bodies with general participation, presuppose much more general, pervasive, and motivationally efficient attitudes of equality than those prevalent today. The inequalities, internalized through the experience of long years of acculturation, and especially through the situation of hierarchical subordination and super-ordination in organizations, will be hard enough to unlearn. To these will have to be added the inequalities produced by the non-uniformity of development. The tension between the increasingly important standard of equality and the forces working against it is likely to grow.

The third field of development of welfare is what I would call social education, using that expression in the sense that we speak of health education—meaning not education of health practitioners, of doctors and nurses, but education of people to protect their own health. In this sense, social education will come to play an increasing and ever larger part in social welfare action. Even today, supposing that practical medicine would one day find itself robbed of the possibility of surgery, of the possibility of applying drugs, including antibiotics, we would find that not much more would be left of medicine than health education. In the social field we are not very far from a similar situation. The surgery and drugs which we apply sometimes have shown dangerous side effects—they have not in practice confirmed that we really know yet how to use them. So we will have to give greater place to social education. What I mean by social education is perhaps a little unorthodox. I would think that what was the standard education of the social worker twenty years ago should, twenty years from now, be the standard education for every person. Instead of teaching civics or some kind of ideological commitment to one side or another, we will teach people how they function in society, what makes them tick, what puts them under stress, what makes problems for them. This kind of general knowledge—and already today this is general knowledge —would have to be taught systematically to everybody, and this will be an important task of welfare.

The practical learning and acceptance of equality is a part of the new concept of welfare. The methods will tend to be composite. General measures promoting equality of condition, mass action teaching equality through actual co-operation, social education in a variety of forms, will go together with a patient building of the new institutional structures implying the solution of innumerable technical problems which are today difficult even to foresee. At the same time the "marginal" traditions of social welfare will possibly come to life again in the task of the treatment of offenses and offenders against equality, or in specialized programmes to promote the well being of groups with a traditionally depressed status and, possibly, to develop a new and expanded ideology to correspond to the changing realities of the situation.

The stresses on a large number of individuals are increased by the political changes that are now unfolding. The traumatic impact of violent political upheaval, however progressive its results, the dangers of concentration of political power often inherent in efforts at accelerated development, and particularly the chilling experience of organizational society are among the main factors producing these stresses. Particularly the situation in large organizations demonstrates to people for the first time not only that co-operation at a technical task is possible without a corresponding community of interests, but that organizations can be turned into instruments of interest domination against their own members. Co-operation is no longer identical with interest-coalition, as it was with pre-organizational arrangements. The resulting feelings of loneliness and of being only a "cog in the machine" are among the principal strains of industrial society.

The political tasks of the future, however, are likely to exceed by far the stresses of the past. The problems of deconcentrating the dangerous agglomerations of political power, of breaking up the structures through which emotions aroused by conflicts of interests were brought to their highest points of intensity, and then of building the new structures for the constant adjustment of diverging interests, for social control without social domination, for free co-operative action—these are tasks which today can be glimpsed only in their barest outline. It will be the responsibility of welfare activity, even if not of social work in the narrow sense of the word, to help in setting up the self-regulating social mechanisms of the future. Take, for example, social security systems, which today are in their most primitive stages. They are based on a very primitive actuarial mathematical principle derived from social insurance systems, but this is completely inadequate to deal with the highly complex problems which, let us say, a national health service or any nation-wide insurance system poses. We have not yet solved these technical problems. To solve them will be a task for the future.

Today already, with social welfare as a subsidiary activity and general welfare as an aim of policy, the problem arises of the possible conflict between institutionalized welfare goals and actual needs of the individual. Welfare is "objectified," and the institutionalized pattern of welfare values is, in a way, imposed on the possibly varying pattern of human needs. This problem has been highlighted particularly by the various definitions of social welfare and social work as "adaptation." Even if the mutual character of adaptation is stressed—individual to society and environment to people—the question remains open how far can institutions adapt people to their requirements without limiting their freedom in an unacceptable way? In the institutional structure of the future this will be a question of basic importance. The greater autonomy of freely co-operating individuals will make them less tolerant towards externally imposed values of whatever character.

To summarize, as social treatment of marginal cases and situations becomes more specialized and present social work knowledge more general, the main attention of a "will to welfare," under conditions of the possible universal satisfaction of material needs, may concentrate on devising measures to neutralize the dysfunctional consequences of social change, to promote equality, and to build new deconcentrated forms of human co-operation. In becoming a generally accepted goal of society, welfare is thus the primary rational content of social action.

MALCOLM S. ADISESHIAH

Welfare in Economic Thought

Welfare in Economic Action

MALCOLM S. ADISESHIAH

Deputy Director-General, UNESCO

Dr. Adiseshiah graduated in economics from the University of Madras, later taking his Doctorate in banking and currency at the London School of Economics and King's College, Cambridge. For six years he lectured at the University of Calcutta, and for ten years was Head of the Department of Economics, University of Madras, during which period he was a member of the group of economists who developed the first Ten-Year Plan for the Industrialization of India. Dr. Adiseshiah was Director of UNESCO's Technical Assistance Programme 1950–1955 and Assistant Director-General 1955–1963. He is the fourth Deputy Director-General of UNESCO since the organization was established in London in 1945.

Welfare in Economic Thought:
Some Micro-Economic Propositions

If the deductions do not agree with the facts, Madam Hypothesis can go to blazes.—*V. Pareto*

It is not wonder [which is the starting-point of philosophy], but rather the social enthusiasm which revolts from the sordidness of mean streets and the joylessness of withered lives, that is the beginning of economic science.—*A. C. Pigou*

WELFARE HAS PROVIDED THE FOUNDATION for much of economic analysis and thought. It has taken different avatars at different points in time and history. The outer shell has been coated and re-coated with sugar and icing, but the inner kernel has remained intact. Welfare dominates economic analysis to the point where it is part of the warp and woof of things economic. It appears as wealth (Adam Smith), as pleasure or happiness (J. Bentham), as utility (A. C. Pigou), as value and price (Ricardo), as money or real income (Keynes), as ophelimity (Croce), as aesthetic realization and creative art (Marx), as the, or a, state of equilibrium (Walras; Marshall) as the, or an, optimum (Bergson; Robbins), as the preferred or chosen position (Pareto; Little), as development and growth (Rostow; Lewis; Myint). Within all these varying and various reflections of welfare in economics, I think three facets of the prism should be distinguished. The first is the attempt to describe, to understand, to seek and search out the laws that characterize men in one particular slice of human life, "in the ordinary

business of life," whether it be Robinson Crusoe's or that undertaken on the island of Mauritius, whether that of the representative
firm or of "Milorg."[1] The second facet leads beyond this stage of
description, understanding, and analysis, to an enquiry into the
bases of these various embodiments of welfare—What is wealth?
Whence is happiness? Should this be of value? Can one move from
one position of optimum to another, through a more equitable distribution of income? Can the preferred positions of two individuals
or groups take into account the balancing or compensation of
increased pain and disutility caused to one and added pleasure and
happiness accruing to another? On what other bases than those
usually called economic are growth rates dependent? And it is at this
point that we begin to glimpse the third facet of welfare. Economics
is concerned with the ordinary business of life in a somewhat narrow
and limited sense. It is usually delimited to those sectors which can
be brought under the measuring rod of money or some other such
quantitative criterion. If man's life, even in its ordinary business,
is not so limited, then man himself, in all his plenitude and
unfathomable depths, cannot be comprehended unless economics
takes its place alongside the other social and human sciences—
ethics, aesthetics, psychology, jurisprudence, sociology, history,
anthropology, linguistics, and philosophy—and becomes part of a
total synthesis, on the basis of which alone can recommendations
be formulated, policies established, and action pursued.

It is the first facet—that of describing, of understanding, of dis-
covering, the relationship between human actions, as seen in consumption, production, savings, income, and trade—which reflects
the largest part of the economist's universe of discourse. What is
common to all these many-sided relationships is their regularity—
the regular, repetitive manner in which they occur—or seem to
occur. This, of course, is the hall-mark of all science, from quantum
mechanics and cell biology to astronomy and oceanography. The
apparent daily rising of the sun, the seeming fortnightly waning of
the moon, the obvious nightly moving of the planets, have the same
characteristic—their regular, repetitive behaviour, which led to the

[1]Short for "military organization," as used by Kenneth Ewart Boulding, "The
World War Industry as an Economic Problem" in Emile Benoit and Kenneth
Ewart Boulding, eds., *Disarmament and the Economy* (New York: Harper and
Row, 1963), p. 7.

theory that these bodies attract one another. This profound truth was based on extending the law of gravity, observed on this planet, to the movement of the celestial bodies. But we must recall that these mathematical relationships which we perceive to occur regularly, are in fact hypotheses, subject, although to a somewhat less degree, to the same reserves which must be expressed towards the hypotheses advanced so fearlessly by Edmond Rostand's cock, that it was his own crowing every morning that caused the sun to rise. For hypotheses in science have never quite avoided this pitfall; scientific laws are no more than theories, however working or workable, and have to allow for a margin of error. It is by maximizing this margin, by quantifying the imperfections of the law, that the science of astronomy has progressed, and as much of its advance today is attributed to its original hypotheses as to its known imperfections and measured lacunae.[2] The quantification of much of economic data—of national income, international trade, growth rates, etc.—find their valid use and rightful application only in so far as their error margins are computed with even greater precision.

Looking at man's welfare from this point of view, it will be noticed that he is continually striving to reach in all his actions a position of preference, a point of optimum, where, to use shorthand, he would be better off at some point in relation to the amount of goods and services he consumes, the quantity and kind of work he performs, and the savings he makes for future consumption. This is an elemental fact of welfare which can be tested by observation. As a young boy, I used to watch my parents' daily actions with considerable fascination. My father thought he had a penchant for bargaining, and I soon realized that he never bought anything— linen textile to be worn as our clothes, or a basket of mangoes for our summer food—unless the seller reduced his price by 25 per cent. My mother, on the other hand, did not like bargaining and was known to all to prefer fixed prices. The result was that, when

[2]Henri Poincaré, *Les méthodes nouvelles de la mécanique céleste* (New York: Dover Publications, 1957). Discussed by V. Pareto, "On the Economic Principle: a Reply to Benedetto Croce," translated from the Italian "Sul Principio Economico," *Giornale degli Economisti*, I (1901), pp. 131–8; in "On the Economic Principle: A Correspondence between B. Croce and V. Pareto," *International Economic Papers*, no. 3 (London and New York: Macmillan Co., 1953), pp. 197– 207.

the shopkeepers saw my father, they would mark up the article—linen which was 1 rupee a yard would be offered to him for 2 rupees, and after hard bargaining would be bought by my father for 1½ rupees. My mother would go to the same shop some time later and purchase the same linen at 1 rupee per yard. Both my parents felt that they were in the position where they could not be better off by any other course of action. And there were similar facts with regard to postponement of present consumption. My father was a great saver and my mother was steeped in acts of charity, and both were in the same position of feeling themselves in a preferred position, only for my father it was putting away the rupee for the future house that he was to build, and for my mother it was giving away one rupee to a needy friend. There was the same kind of balance—stemming from different subjective criteria—as between work and leisure. My father, after a hard day's work in the University, insisted on personally supervising the contractor, who built our house at the cost of 40,000 rupees. My mother later built a similar house by choosing a good architect, and staying at home, at a cost of 35,000 rupees. I realized even in those days that, although my father paid 5,000 rupees more, despite his personal supervision of the contractor, he felt himself to be in a position that was no worse off than my mother's; my parents' choice had been between various alternatives of work and leisure and these were the important and determining elements.

One object of economic analysis is to study what conditions are necessary and/or sufficient in order that all three elements which make up man's daily life, consumption, production, and saving, are at a point of optimum, above or below which he will be worse off. This study and analysis of when and how individuals and groups are better off is worthwhile provided one remembers that, because human motivations are complex, only a small part of what makes up human welfare is involved.

This optimum, this state of being better off which the individual or the group aims at, is the kind of micro-economic analysis which might well be approached in easy stages. For the sake of simplicity, we shall eschew the usual mathematical tools, with consequent loss of some precision and exactitude. In the interest of clarity, we will assume that there are no important or violent changes in the environment, in population, in tastes, in the variety and, in the initial stages, the quantity of goods and services, and in the means of producing them and in their distribution. Under these conditions, when we have a fixed amount of goods and services, the individual is better off when he examines carefully the various alternative uses and combinations confronting him and chooses that distribution of his resources between these various combinations which he feels puts him in the best possible position. It will now be possible to elaborate a series of propositions that are derived from welfare—propositions that seem tautologous, but which both describe and govern our daily actions.

The first proposition relates to consumption—that people get the most out of their limited resources when they distribute these resources among their various uses in such a way that, at the margin, one resource can be replaced by another. This can be seen when we look at a man in a community as a consumer—as a person who enjoys life by using up a certain amount of goods and services to meet his various and varying needs. He will then so choose his goods and services that, at the margin, it is all the same to him whether one unit of a good is replaced by one unit of another good, and when this rate of replacement is the same for all individuals in the group or community. This is usually demonstrated in the familiar box diagram which shows, in relation to the curves, that no movement from the tangency position will place the two persons in a more preferred position. And what is so demonstrated for two persons engaged in buying and selling and consumption of two goods, is equally true for any number of persons and any number of goods. Thus, at the margin, the rate of preference between any two goods for any individual is accurately reflected by the price ratios of those goods.

Let us assume that our consumer prefers apples to oranges, that is, he would pay more for one apple than for one orange, but that in the market oranges are say twice as dear as apples. Then our consumer will buy apples up to the point at which he would be prepared to exchange two apples for one orange, because up to that point he rates apples more highly than the market. It will be similar with all other individuals. It can be demonstrated that this first condition can only be fulfilled when every consumer faces the same price for each product, as otherwise there would be scope for improving the allocation of goods among consumers. Thus my father and mother would both have been "better off" if, say, through an intermediary, my mother sold her cloth to my father at 1.12 rupees (1.5 less than 25 per cent). Differences in tastes are reflected not in different prices, but in different quantities purchased at the given price.

The second proposition relates to the work each person has to do. Individuals and groups aim at attaining a similar optimum position with regard to the quantity and kind of work done and the leisure time available. Here each person will aim at equating at the margin the amount of leisure he would like with the extra amount of work he would otherwise perform. This is obvious, for otherwise he will be better off by doing a little more work and having a little less leisure. I am assuming, of course, that there are choices—shades of my father and his house-building!! And so for the community as a whole, there is a similar substitutability between work and leisure on the one hand, and wages, regarded as returns to the work of the different individuals—whether seen as individuals, as in primary production, or organized in trade unions. Here then is our second proposition. People get most out of this alternative of work and leisure by equating the rates of their replacement at the margin. An optimum position requires that preferences at the margin, as between work and leisure, should be accurately measured by the returns accruing from such work.

The third proposition refers to savings—which are part of the welfare of the individual and community. What guides the actions of either in savings and in investing such savings? Here again each person tries to equate at the margin his present consumption and future consumption of any given good or service. This means that, at the margin, a sum of money in hand or a fixed deposit in the bank, or a share are substitutable for him—as it was for my father. Whether he saved his money or spent it is determined by price and interest movements, which as in the case of goods and services, so too for bank deposits and shares, should be the same for all individuals in the community. And so emerges our third welfare condition: that individuals will be in the position of optimum when their units of savings and investments are, at the margin, able to be substituted not only among themselves, but even more so in relation to alternative current consumption possibilities. At this point, their rates of preference as between saving and investment, on the one hand, and present consumption, on the other, are accurately reflected by the rate of interest.

The fourth proposition concerns production of goods and services. Here in exploring the make-up of welfare, it is necessary to drop one of our many assumptions—i.e., the existence of a fixed quantity of goods and services and the analysis based on that assumption of human behaviour, leading to optimizing consumption and exchange, work and leisure, savings and investment. For now we must consider what is the optimum position with regard to quantities of goods and services, if these quantities can be increased or decreased. Any given volume of production is the result of the factors employed in producing them—such as land, labour, and capital. Hence optimum production will be attained when the ratio of marginal products of the factors are the same, in all cases where they are employed. This means that, where the ratio is lower in one use, the factors in that use will move out to a higher use. This simple rule of thumb is, of course, subject to many welfare qualifications. In the case of the human factor, labour, there is the complication of the alternatives of work and leisure facing the worker, when a shift from one employment to another is involved, and his likes and dislikes with regard to particular jobs. In the extreme case of the society I was in last summer, which is governed in its daily life by the age-old wisdom: "If ever the urge to work comes over you, just lie down and the feeling will pass away," the alternatives are, of course, never-ending and complex. Further, in moving factors, the substitutability of the ratio of their production at the margin is not the only decisive element. There are the side effects involved, such as decreasing the supply of some other commodity, or adding to the mental confusion or enjoyment accompanying modern advertising, opening up new avenues of employment or diminishing the filth and noise of modern urban life. All this must be weighed in. Further optimum production requires that the price of products be equal to their marginal cost and that the price ratio of products be proportional to their marginal displacement costs. Now in so far as there is a price-marginal cost differential in any product, free competition, so far assumed, is absent. Questions of the public share in the differential, taxation, arise. Also, taking into account the side effects referred to earlier, the possibilities of expanding the production of goods and services which give off positive effects, contracting those that produce negative ones, arise in relation to any welfare criterion.[3]

These changes in the production schedule will involve changes in the distribution of goods and services—as between individuals in the community. These we have so far ignored but can no longer do so. From the point of optimum production and its distribution effects, the welfare concept involves quite a few possibilities, which I can only indicate broadly and without repeating their many qualifications. If production can be increased and no one made worse off as a result, there is here an optimum position. In an extreme case, even if the total volume of production is increased by one good and no one is worse off after this one good comes out, a new optimum will be reached and so on. But now our fourth proposition can be stated. An increase in the volume of the total production of a community, which is brought about either by increasing some goods without decreasing others, or by shifting factors used in their production to sectors in which prices are higher, is an optimum position to the community, provided the share of the goods accruing to the poorer section of the community is not reduced.[4]

The fifth proposition relates to distribution and re-distribution, arising from the limitations and obstacles that face the realization of optimum conditions of consumption, work, savings, and production, that have been elaborated thus far. In dealing with consumption, for instance, we treated people as independent units whose preferences depended on their individual stocks and their isolated consumption patterns. But individuals in society are interrelated as consumers, so that a preferred position to one or a group of individuals might well involve less preferred positions for others. It might follow that, for society as a whole, some sort of rationing

[3]For further discussion see: R. F. Kahn, "Some Notes on Ideal Output," *Economic Journal*, vol. XLV (March, 1935), pp. 1–35; John Richard Hicks, "The Rehabilitation of Consumers' Surplus," *Review of Economic Studies*, vol. VIII, no. 2 (1940–1), p. 108; E. J. Mishan, "A Survey of Welfare Economics," *Economic Journal*, vol. LXX, no. 278 (June, 1960), pp. 197–265.

[4]See Arthur Cecil Pigou, *The Economics of Welfare* (London: Macmillan and Co. Ltd., 1920), pp. 42–68.

might be needed, as a counter balance. Similarly, earlier assumptions of unchanged and unchanging tastes, perfect knowledge of the future, and time preferences as well as the many-sided effects to work of one individual as compared to another, need to be modified and might then lead to sub-optimum positions for whole groups in society. This means that optimum conditions described so far must be modified from the point of view of distribution, as technically such optima could be attained even with zero incomes for certain individuals or sections in the community.

Again, under certain rather limited conditions, an increase in production will be a preferred position to the community, whether it results from expanding or subsiding those sectors which are functioning under conditions of increasing returns to the factors employed, and taxing and in other ways curtailing those sectors which are functioning under the opposite condition, i.e., of diminishing returns to the factors invested. More precisely stated, the welfare of a community might involve expanding those activities and industries where the ratios of price to marginal cost are above the average and contracting those whose ratio of price to marginal cost is below, leaving aside the side effects of these activities and industries. This leads to the presumption, again under certain conditions, that any form of further direct taxation which replaces indirect taxes, certain public utility undertakings such as roads, railways, bridges, water supply, parks, and museums, which are financed from direct taxes, and/or whose price is below marginal cost, will have similar effects on distribution. In fact, in the case of some of these public utilities where marginal cost is zero or near nil, their utilization is free, as in the case of parks, roads and water, bridges and museums, in most cases. In the case where a public enterprise has positive costs, if its price structure is to cover its total costs, then from the point of view of optimum distribution, it must be multi-priced—charging a higher price for the richer members of the community and a lower one for the poorer.

This reasoning could be even further generalized from the point of view of welfare. In extreme cases, if any gainful economic organization of the community causes gains to some of its members and losses to others, from the point of view of distribution, through an appropriate pricing, subsidizing, or taxing policy, the losers tend to be compensated for their losses, particularly if they are the poorer sections of the community. With this, the fifth proposition can be summarily stated. Any of the situations (set forth above) which result in increasing the net share of the poorer section of the community, without diminishing the total volume of production for the community, is part of the community's optimum position.

The sixth proposition relates to national income. Welfare considerations lead further to the examination of the make-up of national income, and in what ways again can the national income for a community be considered to be in an optimum position. At this point a further assumption so far made must be dropped— namely, that the factors used in the total volume of production are a fixed quantity. Now we should recognize a certain amount of elasticity in the supply of factors which go into the production of the total volume of goods and services. Further, the implicit assumption referred to and modified to some extent earlier, namely the absence of free competition and the presence of various forms of monopolistic organization and restrictive associations in the units of production, is now given force. In computing the national income and making inter-temporal comparisons of the national income, a well-worn friend, in the form of the appropriate index number, is normally used—with due caution engendered by all that has been said and written on unreliability and the large margins of approximation in all social accounting and economic statistics.[5] The index

$$\sum P_2 Q_2 \geqslant \sum P_2 Q_1 \quad \text{or} \quad \sum P_1 Q_1 < \sum P_1 Q_2$$

simply states that value of the national income in Period 2 is not less than the income in Period 1, valued at P_2 (i.e., current) prices, and that value of the national income in Period 1 is less than the real income in Period 2, valued at P_1 (i.e., base year) prices. It means the national income not being less in the second period, the community, given no adverse distribution effects, is in an optimum position at that point. This is tautological.

But the composition of the national income is quite another matter. It includes individual goods and services consumed by

[5]See Simon Kuznets, "On the Valuation of Social Income—Reflections on Professor Hicks' Article," *Economica*, Feb. 1948, pp. 1–16, and May 1948, pp. 116–31; and Paul A. Samuelson, "Evaluation of Real National Income," *Oxford Economic Papers*, new series, vol. II, no. 1, (Jan., 1950), pp. 1–29.

persons. It includes collective goods and services which are at the disposal of the individual at varying prices, ranging from η to zero. It includes factors, labour, and capital, which can be expanded in accordance with similar propositions to those set forth concerning an expansion in the production of goods, provided distribution effects are not worsened. And then the whole problem of obsolescence, upkeep, and replacement of capital, so that the computation of national income includes such parts of the total output as represent a net addition to the community's capital, whether under public or private auspices, must be taken into account. In this manner, it will be possible to reckon in the national income all savings in the community from private corporations and public sources and a quantity vastly more difficult, the production potential of the community at different points of time.[6] This means that the national income is computed by adding disposable income, that is wages and salaries, interest, profits, minus direct taxes, plus transfers, savings, and free public services. This latter includes the services of police, jails, justice, and the whole defence sector. The place of these last two sectors in national income, and the optimum analysis that they give rise to, is a highly interesting subject in itself. For our limited purposes here, however, the police, jails, and justice sector is treated in similar terms to that of any public enterprise, financed out of tax revenue, providing a negative–positive function, in prevention of law violation and in law enforcement. The defence sector is quite another issue and is more realistically treated when we pass from the problems of the closed to those of the open community. The sixth proposition which thus emerges is that any increase in the measured national income, provided there is no worsening of its distribution, can be taken as a preferred position for the community.

The seventh proposition emerges out of an analysis of international trade. For this it is necessary to look at the economic relations between one group or nation and another, in the matter of production and distribution of goods and services. The rationale for international trade and the gains and losses from it are part of the optimum propositions under examination. Let us suppose that a

[6]Alfred Marshall, *Principles of Economics: An Introductory Volume*, (8th ed.; London: Macmillan and Co., Ltd., 1961), pp. 60–9, 432–5.

country has reached all the various positions of optima that have been so far analysed. When such a country then comes into relation with one or all other countries, unless an extraordinary coincidence occurs, the prices of a number of goods in the first country will be higher or lower than those of similar goods in the other country or countries. Then trade—the international exchange of goods— follows. In fact, in the domestic optimum of production referred to earlier, no account was taken of the fact that some commodities may be produced in excess of domestic demand, for export pur- poses, and conversely that the excess of demand over domestic production in some lines of production will be met by imports. An optimum representing national self-sufficiency in any full economic sense means that the nation is in a less preferred position than it would be through moving to a position where its domestic imbal- ances are corrected through exports and imports. This is the simple and historic argument for freedom of international trade—a system of international exchanges which enables each country to enjoy the many-sided advantages of international specialization, in accord- ance with the principle of comparative costs. Canada can make not only jet engines but also textiles at a lower cost than Hong Kong. But because Canada has a relatively greater cost advantage over Hong Kong in making jet engines than in manufacturing textiles, the optimum for the two countries involves Canada devoting its resources to jet engines and Hong Kong to textiles, which are then exchanged for each other. Thus, after trade has taken place, the optimum position is again reached at all levels. After the trade equilibrium position is attained as in the pre-trade optimum posi- tion, no changes will make anyone better off.

This optimum position for a country involving free international trade derives its finest exemplification from nineteenth-century Europe, with the United Kingdom as the dynamic economic centre of the world. With the fifty-year start given to it by the industrial revolution, within thirty years of the latter half of the nineteenth century, its overall import coefficient roughly doubled from 18 to 36 per cent as a result of free trade; and at the end of the nineteenth century and beginning of the twentieth, the United Kingdom accounted for 36 per cent of the world exports of manufactures and 27 per cent of the world imports of primary commodities—a position never before or ever again attained by anyone. Here is the classical case and vindication of free trade. It is not surprising, therefore, that for a large body of thinking men and women, even today, the optimum position for every country is to be found in what would follow from the removal of the obstacles which impede the free play of the forces of international trade and its basis in comparative costs. The regional groupings in the European Economic community, the European Free Trade Association, in Western Europe, and the Council for Mutual Economic Assistance in Eastern Europe, although a long way from the classical doctrine of free trade, are rightly grounded on the certain firm base of economic homogeneity—which being absent for all countries everywhere, is the main case against free trade and any optimal arrangement that may, in theory, ensue from it.

But even in its heyday, the optimum, as a function of free international trade, admitted of important exceptions. The well-known infant industry argument indicates that a position of optimum will be reached, after a temporary passage through a less preferred position, when the relative costs of the industry in question will be reduced, as the infant grows up. New equations of production and consumption and relative prices will then have been attained. A second and even more powerful argument may be advanced from the point of view of distribution. In certain cases, a carefully worked-out tariff policy can bring about an optimum position in terms of employment, in the supply and distribution of goods and services in demand by the poorer section of the community, so that the community as a whole is better off in the post-tariff era than in the pre-tariff era. The seventh proposition resulting from this analysis of international trade may now be formulated. International trade—free or protected—is a condition for a nation's placing itself in a preferred position. Free international trade is a condition for achieving a world optimum. There is a case from the point of distribution of incomes between various members and sections of the community for the presumption that a carefully constructed post-tariff optimum is one which is, on the whole, in its interests.

It is at this point that, at the cost perhaps of a slight digression, the place of the defence industry in the economic welfare of the community, and its contribution to the optimum position which each country aims at, might be briefly examined. That the defence sector has its economic implications is obvious. On the basis of available data, all countries together seem to be spending today 140,000 million dollars annually on defence—a sum which represents more than three-fourths of the national income of all developing countries. In the trade and aid context, my estimate on the basis of available information is that the international movements in this sector may be valued annually at 4 to 5 billion dollars during the last two decades. (I admit a rather large margin of error in this estimate, as so much of the information is "classified.") This whole subject has of course been extensively treated elsewhere, and I shall limit myself to a few observations relevant to my theme. The defence sector, like every other sector producing capital or consumer goods, operates on a cost accounting basis, competes for the available supply of labour and manpower skills in the nation, and like some of the public enterprises depends on tax revenue. The main point of departure, however, is that the output of the defence sector today is, in this age of nuclear weaponry and delivery, not only contributing nothing to welfare, but is in the position of contributing positively to the ill-fare of every nation. I am not here referring to the withdrawal of resources from the production of capital and consumer goods that the existence of the defence sector involves, and that so many of the excellent United Nations studies on the social and economic consequences of disarmament highlight. I am not referring to the sacrifices imposed on nations—particularly the powerful industrial nations—caused by this annual investment of the major part of 140,000 million dollars in the defence sector, involving the withdrawal of a potentially equivalent amount from other productive uses. I am not even thinking of the potential ill-fare that might be caused by the sleeping sentry. I am referring to the startling conclusion that the highest scientists have reached, both in the United States and the Soviet Union, that "there is no technical solution to the dilemma of steadily increasing military power and steadily decreasing national security."[7] Under these conditions, economic analysis can and does indicate that, following

7Jerome B. Weisner and Herbert F. York, "National Security and the Nuclear-Test Ban," *Scientific American*, vol. 211, no. 4 (Oct., 1964), pp. 27–35.

the classical market analysis of bargaining—in this case not as between a buyer and seller, but as between two defence sectors, who are each buyers and sellers at the same time—it is possible to move towards a long-range optimum situation for each country, leading to graduated but complete disarmament, in each stage of which, as in the case of market preferences, each party would be better off than before. From the point of view of welfare and various preferred positions that we have been analysing, in our nuclear age, I would go even further in expressing my agreement with the position that, again from the point of view of the cost benefit relationship, "there is a strong case for unilateral disarmament, as there was a case for personal disarmament in the age of the colt."[8]

The eighth proposition arises from planning. Welfare criteria point to long-term considerations, hindsight and farsightedness in economic analysis and action. It is at this point that planning as a tool or technique to reach optimum position or positions for the community needs consideration. There are wide differences as to the meaning and content of planning, and, in all economic literature, probably no other politico-economic phenomenon arouses more violent emotions—proceeding in most cases, from deep-seated social convictions. Planning in this context, however, is used to refer to the setting of goals or targets, and the elaboration of means whereby these targets may be achieved. The former is outside, the latter within, the economist's universe of discourse. For the Fifth Plan, covering the years 1966–70, which was approved by the National Assembly of France on December 1, 1964, the planners recommended a 4.5 per cent annual rate of economic growth as the target. The Assembly and the Government, however, decided that this was not good enough and instructed the economists—the Commissariat au Plan—to revise the plan on the basis of a 5 per cent annual growth. In the complex technological world of today, the movement towards optima involves the planning of targets and goals—whether these be recommended by a council of economic advisers of the U.S. type, a planning commission of the French or Indian type, or a Gosplan body of the Soviet type, their final determination being in the hands of political authority. When it comes to the elaboration of means—complex, innumerable, highly

[8]Kenneth E. Boulding, in *Disarmament and the Economy*, p. 27.

decentralized, and localized, a matter in which the economist has a major, if not the determinant, role to play, there is a wide variety of choices to be faced and no generalization can be made of what constitutes the desiderata towards the optimum. Two general situations in any system of planning may be noted. First, the general criteria for the optimum which demonstrated that prices must be equal or as nearly equal (depending on existing technical market perfections) to marginal costs, might require public intervention in some sectors of production. In the kind of production situation, which is to be found in every country, in some sectors, where a few large units operate and have the power to divorce price rather seriously from marginal cost, state intervention, carefully planned, is an assurance that the optimum condition of price-marginal cost equation is realized. This condition may be generalized, whatever may be the political or economic structure under consideration. If it can be achieved by the free play of the market, then that is indicated; if it can be achieved only by public ownership and management, then that would be required. In between there are many alternative forms of intervention which planning techniques must encompass.

The second area which calls for similar action is where the community has decided that certain goods should not be available; where certain goods can only be consumed simultaneously or collectively; where a given aggregate magnitude of investment in a particular sector is an absolute requirement for the community. In these cases, again the attaining of the optimum calls for planning of the means in a detailed and regulated manner. The eighth proposition which thus emerges is that the explicit elaboration of the goals and targets to be fixed by political authority, and indeed by society as a whole, and the working out of the detailed means of achieving them, are a function of welfare economics today, and a means of attaining the optimum position which every community strives at.

The eight propositions that have been derived from an analysis of the welfare foundations in economic thought really reduce themselves to three broad conclusions. First, the welfare of the individual, the group and the community—defined in any sense—looked at from the economic point of view, requires that the available resources should be efficiently distributed between various competing uses. Here what is required is forethought, skill, and knowledge, in the allocation of resources, so that the individual, the group and the community are in the most favoured position.

Second, the welfare of the various parties that we have had under examination requires that the optimum be reached by making every effort possible to increase the resources available. This was the main preoccupation of the founding fathers of economic science. They saw the optimum as the resultant of a continual struggle between nature and man, nature with its apparent limits and man with his unlimited possibilities. In the modern technological era, with the assurance that there is no long-term limitation to resources and their use, we are simply going back to this second condition for the optimum—that of bending all our efforts, in every possible manner, to increase available resources.[9]

The third broad conclusion suggested is that the optimum requires a progressive improvement in the distribution of goods and services as between different sectors of society, so that distribution between individuals, groups, and classes, within a community, moves in favour of the poorer and less favoured section, without jeopardizing the efficiency of allocation of resources, which it need not do, and without diminishing the total resources, the aggregate volume of production, which it should not do.

Welfare considerations, as pointed out at the outset, constitute the yardstick by which these conclusions are seen to be in need of further reinforcement. First, the economist is looking at life through a microscope and is seeing through it only a microcosm of an entire organ—vital in itself, but a minutia. That particular microcosm,

[9]Academician N. M. Sissakian (USSR), in his presidential address to the 13th Session of the General Conference of UNESCO, declared:

In the light of present-day achievements in the natural sciences and in technology, the danger—which used to be spoken of, and still unfortunately is in some circles—of exhausting our planet's sources of energy and of the shortage of food resources for mankind, in the face of the increasing growth of population, proves unfounded. All grounds for pessimism on this score have disappeared. . . .

In a world of social and technological progress, the full satisfaction for all times of the food and energy requirements of mankind, the elimination of infectious illness, the conquest of cardio-vascular diseases and cancer, the consequent achievement of unprecedented and zestful longevity and a hitherto unknown flourishing of education, science and culture—all this is becoming no longer a dream but a real likelihood for the not very distant future. 13 C/INF/7, Unesco, Oct. 21, 1964.

further, has no life of its own. It takes on life—considerably changed and modified—when seen in its organic setting. I will only recall here the second and third facets of the impact of welfare on economics, which I have not dealt with except in a cursory manner, when discussing some aspects of distribution, international trade, disarmament and planning. Whether one goes as far as to affirm this inter-relatedness by saying that "economics in fact cannot be dissociated from ethics"[10] or by pointing out that the reality of man's preferences, the content of a country's needs, the ethics of a society's demands are to be found outside of economics, its analysis and description, the point at issue is granted.

This is the point at which the formal analysis of optimum, of choice, of preferred position, has to be corrected by the totality of man's life and outlook, and the real significance of society's demands. In this setting, human wants are not given; choices are not static. Optimum and preferred positions are the result of dynamic and changing needs and situations. I am not able to join in characterizing wants as "the most difficult element to know in a whole system of variables."[11] I will admit, however, that the establishment of optimum through meeting existing wants is only a first exploratory step. Like the door to "my father's house in which there are many mansions," it opens up a whole host of other possibilities and interrelated needs, and to base our analysis merely on preferences and choices of known quantities is like stopping at the entrance to the house. The repetitive character of action and phenomena, on which all scientific analysis is built, is, in the case of man, only the introduction to understanding his behaviour. From repetitive action he moves on to innovative action, from existing and known needs he moves on to building his higher and better wants.

This interrelatedness points to the need to take into account the kind of dynamics of life and society which are not encompassed within the economists' universe of discourse. In the affluent societies,

[10]Ralph George Hawtrey, *Economic Destiny* (London, New York, Toronto: Longmans, Green and Co., 1944), p. 7.
[11]For a more extensive discussion of the nature of "wants" see: Frank H. Knight, *Risk, Uncertainty and Profit* (Boston, New York: Houghton Mifflin Co.; Cambridge: The Riverside Press, 1921; eighth impression 1957), chap. III "The Theory of Choice and of Exchange," pp. 51–93, particularly pp. 51–4, 58–64.

which Europe and North America represent, in this rich one-third of our world, is it really necessary to expend so much effort and concentrate so much of our attention on the examination and analysis of optima and preferred positions, which emerge from grubbing around at the margin. A rich society can only progress further through allowing for wastes in order that it may continue in its affluence. To such a society, equations, arrived at by squeezing out this and adding to that at the margin, are not of decisive importance, because it has passed beyond that particular point. Its preoccupations are of an extra-economic order, such as unplanned leisure and juvenile delinquency, unconcerted development of communication media, and a rhythm and speed of life generally which raises problems of co-operation and friendship, unrelenting pursuit of affluence raising problems of health, physical and mental, and possibly diminishing opportunities for understanding, extending and applying the values by which all men, at all times and everywhere, live   the values of truth, beauty, and goodness.[12]

I can think of no more appropriate call to a school of social work celebrating its fiftieth anniversary than this: to contribute its share in harmonizing and humanizing values, economics, the social structure, and its surroundings—which might eventually lead to that true synthesis of thought and action which will be as comprehensive as life itself. That at least is the moral of this discourse—that all economic thought originates in welfare and is in the end tested by its contribution to welfare.

REFERENCES

A. BERGSON, "A Reformulation of Certain Aspects of Welfare Economics," *Quarterly Journal of Economics,* Feb., 1938.

JOHN MAURICE CLARK, "Preface to Social Economics, *"Essays on Economic Theory and Social Problems* (New York: Farrar & Rinehart, Inc., 1936).

IAN MALCOLM D. LITTLE, *A Critique of Welfare Economics* (Oxford: Clarendon Press, 1950; 2nd ed., 1958).

---

[12]John Kenneth Galbraith. *The Affluent Society* (New York: The New American Library, 1963, Mentor Book; first published by Houghton Mifflin Co., Boston, 1958) pp. 220–7, 259–69.

HLA MYINT, *The Economics of the Developing Countries* (London: Hutchinson and Co., 1964).

WALT WHITMAN ROSTOW, *The Stages of Economic Growth: A Non-Communist Manifesto* (Cambridge: Cambridge University Press, 1960).

UNITED NATIONS, Department of Economic and Social Affairs, *Economic and Social Consequences of Disarmament* (E/3593/Rev. 1) (New York: United Nations, 1962).

UNITED NATIONS, General Assembly, *Report of the United Nations Scientific Committee of the Effects of Atomic Radiation*, General Assembly Official Records: Seventeenth Session, supplement no. 16 (A/5216), (New York: U.N., 1962); also Eighteenth Session (A/5406) (New York: U.N., 1963); Nineteenth Session, supplement no. 14 (A/5814) (New York: U.N., 1964).

Welfare in Economic Action: Some Macro-Economic Conclusions

Damn Economics! Let us build a decent world!—*F. V. Hayek*

We are concerned with the nature and causes of the Poverty of Nations. And do not let us make a mistake in the multiplication table.—*R. G. Hawtrey*

THE IMPORTANCE of production and distribution of goods for all countries and the suggestion that the world's affluent societies need not go grubbing around the margin lead us to some macro-economic considerations which the welfare criteria suggest. If one-third of our world can be described as wealthy and economically developed, the other two-thirds must be described as poverty-stricken and economically developing. The wealthy one-third in Europe, North America, and Australasia has an average per capita income of $1,000 or more, while the poor two-thirds which comprise the countries of Asia, Africa, and Latin America, average per capita incomes of $100 or less.[1] This per capita income yardstick does not really tell the whole story, certainly not the true welfare story, which is our concern. There are simple problems arising from unreliable, incomplete and, in some cases, absent statistics, which make these estimates sometimes no more than "guestimates." There

[1]United Nations Statistical Office, *Per Capita National Product of Fifty-five Countries: 1952–1954* (ST/STAT/SER.E/4, Oct., 1956) (New York, 1957), pp. 7–9.

is the further problem of equating per capita money incomes with per capita real incomes. Mink coats, which are part of real income in the rich cold north, give rise to conundrums in the real income computation of the tropics. There is still another complication arising from the tenuous relationship between the per capita yardstick and levels of living. Levels of living, as defined by the United Nations, comprise health, food consumption and nutrition, education, employment and working conditions, housing, social security, clothing, recreation, and human freedom—the last two vital imponderables not being susceptible of any per capita measurement. Even so the per capita instrument is the only rough and ready measure of the welfare and ill-fare of the individual, of the wealth and poverty of the nations, that is to hand. Its function is primarily one of education and illumination. Its appeal is to the heart and conscience. It sends out an echo on what has been said about distribution and its relation to optimum, as well as to pressing problems of production.

From the point of view of welfare, a less unreliable indicator is probably, in terms borrowed from biology, the rate of growth and development of a country. A country's rate of growth, which is a function of the interrelationship between income, consumption, and investment, may be described as the terms of reference of the race for economic health—we seem to be getting near the welfare concept here—for the programme of economic well-being, which every nation is engaged in today. For the affluent nations, it may be an expression also of the race for economic power; in the case of the poor nations it is an indicator as well as an expression of their desire for higher levels of living.

The rate of growth of the gross domestic product for the decade 1950–60, for the world (excepting socialist countries, whose computation is on a different basis) is 4 per cent. It is 4.4 per cent for developing and 4 per cent for developed countries. The share of the gross domestic product of the latter is 85 per cent and that of the former is 15 per cent. The per capita growth rate (arrived at by dividing G.D.P. by population) is 2.7 per cent for developed and 2.2 per cent for developing countries. The differing rates of growth of the two groups have many facets. But at the outset two common misconceptions about developing countries need to be cleared out of the way. First, their economies are not stagnant, their societies are not "particularistic rather than universalistic."[2] Second, there is a wide margin of difference among them—countries like India and China with a heavy population pressure and a level of industrial and primary production and development differ from an oil-dominated economy like Iraq or such one or few crop economies as those of Nigeria and Senegal. This means that from the point of view of rates of growth, there are some points of convergence between the developed and developing countries, but there are also rather marked differences among the developing countries themselves. The general micro-economic propositions developed apply alike to all countries, rich and poor, developed and developing. The macro-economic considerations which are now set forth refer largely to the developing, low-income, economically poor countries of the world.

In the micro-economic analysis, movements to positions of optimum—of production, price, and income and their interrelationship—have been rightly based on the assumption of an unchanged social and technological framework within which such movements take place. When changes in their relationship were taken into account, even when they resulted from social and institutional conditions, they were considered for the purpose of analysis to result from exogenous factors, which were not themselves subject to examination. Such a methodology was needed, not only to sharpen our economic tools (as happens with all methodology in science) as they were confronting the welfare concept, but also to avoid a mere description of phenomena and a tiresome listing of institutions and their changes. It must also be recalled that we confined analysis for the most part to very short-term or very long-term movements and, in both these cases, taking exogenous factors as given is a realistic assumption. But as we turn to growth and development, there are no exogenous conditions. Now economic analysis concerning growth, as an outcome and indicator of welfare, must integrate the actual social and institutional conditions within which movements towards the optimum take place, right

[2]Terminology used by Talcott Parsons cited in *Social Prerequisites to Economic Growth: Report of an Expert Working Group (Kyrenia, Cyprus, 17–26 April 1963)*, Unesco document UNESCO/SS/38 (Paris, March 23, 1964), p. 6.

inside the traditional input-output models, which are normally based on doses of capital and labour, with a given supply of land and technical knowledge. And so our first conclusion which emerges is this: that in examining development and growth, particularly for low-income countries, the forces behind technical knowledge and the technological framework of the country, and the highly sophisticated aggregates of capital and labour for that country, have to be examined and broken down. The light they throw on growth problems is an inherent part of the welfare indicator, which is our concern.

The rate of growth so conceived is a function of savings and investments in a country. It is generally estimated that, for all countries, the investment required for growth involves a minimal saving of 10 to 12 per cent of the national income. A historical study of the developed countries during the 50 to 100 years—covering the before-and-after years of their take-off points—is one evidence of this 10 to 12 per cent indicator. It can also be tested by the generally accepted capital-income or investment-output ratio of 3:1.

In general, this ratio is high in housing, railways, communications, electric generation and supply, and rather low in agriculture, manufacturing, and mining. The rate of savings in the low-income countries varies widely. In Asia, it is around 10 per cent of the national income, leaving aside war-torn areas like Korea, Vietnam, and Laos. In Africa, it ranges from 5 per cent of the national income in the case of French-speaking countries, to about 10 per cent in the case of the English-speaking countries. In Latin America it varies over a wide range, averaging around 15 per cent. This general picture of the developing countries suggests that the savings targets for the 5 percenters should move to 10, for the 10 percenters should move to 15, and for the 15 percenters should move to 20. What institutional and social changes are needed for the attainment of these savings targets,[3] particularly for countries nearing, in varying ways, the take-off stage—countries like India, UAR, Brazil, and Mexico—are cardinal issues posed by welfare criteria.

Higher rates of savings can be attained by various institutional and

[3]William Arthur Lewis, *The Theory of Economic Growth* (London: George Allen and Unwin Ltd., 1955), pp. 225–44.

social devices. In the United Kingdom, in the pre-trade union days of the industrial revolution, wages were kept down and the source of the high rate of savings was the thrifty businessman. This provides no guide, as welfare rules out such distribution effects. In the USSR, savings were added to, through compulsory farm deliveries and the general price structure and policy followed by the authorities —measures that involved heavy sacrifices which again, from the point of view of welfare, are not advocated. In some Latin American countries, a programme of sustained inflation helps in reducing consumption sharply and increases savings, although it brings with it a sub-optimum allocation of resources and balance of payments problems. There is also the normal taxation method—in its various forms, on domestic and export products. For the developing countries, the rate of savings, which is a cardinal element in their growth and development, will, in the end, depend on the income level, the pattern of income distribution, the inducement to private corporations and firms, as well as public enterprises, the tax structure and such ingenious devices as social insurance and general insurance. Hence our second conclusion is that low-income countries, at varying stages of development, must make use of all possible incentives and existing and new institutions to promote a rate of savings ranging from 10 to 20 per cent of their national income, depending on their particular place in the development ladder.

The rate of savings and investment is, in developing countries, interrelated with problems of primary production. Excluding petroleum production, the percentage of primary production in the gross domestic product for developing countries is around 50 per cent, and more than 50 per cent of the labour force of these countries is engaged in this sector. The share of agricultural production in the gross domestic product valued at current factor cost varies from around 4 per cent for countries like the U.S.A., U.K., and Sweden, to around 60 per cent for countries like Uganda, Tanganyika, and Sudan. A detailed table setting forth this relationship for some 70 countries is attached (see Appendix), from which many illuminating correlations may be derived. First of all, the table does bring out the key role of the agricultural sector for developing countries.

This sector provides food for the population, which is growing today at the rate of 2 per cent. It is the consumer of a large part of the finished and other goods produced by the manufacturing sector. With the exception of large and heavily populated countries like India, it provides the main export base for the low-income countries. Somewhere around 50 per cent of the world primary exports are from these countries. Further, improvement in the input-output ratio of agriculture is needed for raising per capita incomes in developing countries. Population growth in these areas is high, as is the income elasticity of demand. Hence, the input-output ratio in agriculture has direct relationship, positive or negative, on their growth rates. Despite the basic importance of this sector, the agricultural growth rates registered in these countries are not only low but have accompanying attributes of slowness and sluggishness. It is this which, in large part, accounts for the poverty of these countries. The world growth rate in the primary sector, over the past thirty years, is 1.4 per cent, while that for the manufacturing sector is more than double that rate—3.4 per cent. Thus while the agricultural sector expanded by less than 60 per cent during this period, the manufacturing industrial sector grew by 300 per cent. Probably there is no more urgent problem in growth economics than that of the agricultural sector shedding its present sluggishness and becoming an agent and a contributory force to development.

In considering how a more satisfactory growth rate in the agricultural sector could be attained, the distinction as between low-income countries made earlier assumes particular importance. The basic situation to bear in mind is that the agricultural area in Asia is 1.5 acres per person; in Latin America 6.9 acres per person; and in Africa 10.6 acres per person.[4] For Asian countries with a heavy rural population density, the main method for expanding agricultural production and accelerating the growth rate of this sector must thus be the raising of agricultural productivity, through appropriate changes in agricultural techniques and organization, through improvements in irrigation, transport, credit facilities, extension services, fertilizers, improved and new seeds, and even

---

[4]*World Population and Resources: A Report by P.E.P.* (London: Political and Economic Planning, 1955), p. 50.

more urgently, through wisely and widely expanded education and training facilities.

During India's first two plan periods, for instance, the 5 per cent growth rate averaged in the primary sector was the combined result of land reform instituted by the 14 state governments and the application of many of the measures just referred to, alongside a serious lag in the provision of adequate education and training opportunities. I believe some part of the falling off of the productivity curve of this sector during the current third plan period (some computations have it as low as 2 per cent) may be ascribed to the insufficient investment in education and training in the earlier plan periods. A comparative table indicating the number of agricultural science students by continent in relation to (*a*) the total number of students enrolled in all faculties of universities and colleges, and (*b*) the total population, shows how far India is lagging behind in agricultural education and training:

	Total no. of students	Agricultural science students	Agricultural science students as percentage of all students	No. of agricultural science students per million population
Africa	129,900	7,100	5.4	50
Latin America	490,100	9,800	2.0	55
Asia (excluding India and China)	632,600	25,200	4.0	66
India	833,400	9,600	1.1	24
Europe (part of)	706,100	14,700	2.0	72

The relative ratios show India to be lagging behind all the other groups both in terms of the ratios of agricultural student enrolment to total students and agricultural students to total population. This lag is even more serious if it is noted that the group called Europe covers Austria, Belgium, Denmark, Finland, France, West Germany, Netherlands, Norway, Switzerland, and the United Kingdom —countries which are among the most industrialized in the world.[5] During the three plan periods, Indian agricultural education investment shows a downward trend; whatever new investments in

[5]Adam Curle, *Educational Strategy for Developing Societies: A Study of Educational and Social Factors in Relation to Economic Growth* (London: Tavistock Publications, Ltd., 1963), p. 101.

agricultural human resources were undertaken traces back to bilateral foreign assistance—notably that from the United States.

Further, there is also need for increasing such infra-structural investments in rural area development as electrification, rural industries, medical, and sanitation services, etc. Indeed, these are necessary adjuncts which round off the improvements in agriculture and its allied services and in education, which have been dealt with at some length. This overall approach, which simultaneously deals with these many interrelated rural problems, may best be described as regional development, rather than rural development.

For countries at the other end of the rural population density scale, such as those in Africa and, to some extent, in Latin America, expansion of agricultural productivity can be achieved to some degree simply first by the normal market incentives, i.e., an adequate price structure, leading to an increasing flow of consumer goods to the farming population, as well as by land reform and the other measures referred to in relation to the first group of countries. The land tenure problem, however, is in as urgent need of solution in Latin America as it is in Asia, where surveys show that 90 per cent of first-quality land is in the hands of 10 per cent of the owners, with accompanying under- or mal-utilization of the best land. And for all regions, agricultural wastages resulting from out-moded technology have more than their rightful share in slowing down agricultural growth and expansion. Poor technology in storage, processing and transportation leads to a loss of about 10 per cent of the annual agricultural production of the developing countries, going up to as much as 20 per cent for some countries.[6] Thus the third conclusion which emerges is that, to accelerate the growth rate of the low-income countries, considered as a movement towards an optimum position for each of them, agricultural production should be rapidly expanded through a combination of land reform action, the provision of positive economic incentives, and the many measures which improve technology, credit and marketing, together with an adequate education and training programme for this sector.

[6]Inter-American Committee for Agricultural Development, *Meeting of High-Level Experts in Agricultural Problems, Held in Washington, D.C.*, Oct. 9–13, 1961 (Washington, D.C.: Pan American Union, General Secretariat of the Organization of American States), pp. 44–5.

This rate of growth in primary production in developing countries must be considered in relation to the rate at which their population is increasing. What evidence there is at hand shows that, before their economies were opened up after the industrial revolution, the population position of these countries was relatively stable, their birth and death rates being equated at a high annual average of 4 per cent. With their contact with Europe came improved means of communication and transport, making possible a relatively even distribution of food. These improvements bring about a situation in which, as a finance minister in India, referring to this factor, once declared in the early years of this century, the budget of the government, like the economy of the country, is no longer a gamble in the monsoons, and the more even distribution of food can be taken to reduce the death rate by 1 per cent. The introduction of public health measures, particularly in the control and eradication of communicable diseases, like malaria, can be taken to reduce the death rate by a further 1 per cent. Finally, the development of modern medical and hospital services, in particular the system of preventive medicine, could involve a further reduction of the death rate by 1 per cent. If all three factors operate in a developing country, then with the birth-rate still at 4 per cent and the death-rate reduced to 1 per cent, the net rate of population growth becomes 3 per cent. In my own life-time, the expectation of life in my country, India, has more than doubled, from a little under 20 in the 1910's, to a little over 40 today. Most developing countries have gone through the first stage fairly fully and are nearing completion of the second stage, so that their net population growth rate is 1½ to 2 per cent. Some of them are well into the third stage, involving them in annual population increases of well above 2 per cent. Today, Latin America is experiencing the fastest population increase at a rate of 2.4 per cent, with Asia and Africa rapidly reaching the 2 per cent mark. The seriousness of the problems presented by these rates of population increases, for welfare and optimum positions, have been well-known since the times of Malthus. The pressure on food supply is unbearably increased in the short run, as the annual reports of the Director-General of F.A.O. repeatedly emphasize. India, with a population of 438 million, which was increasing at the rate of 5 million per year in the 1950's, is increasing in the 1960's at the rate of 8 million annually. Endowed with what can be a large domestic market, when the income level of her people rises to an adequate scale, India presents a favourable environment for large investments in heavy capital goods industries and their attendant economies of scale. But the large investment in heavy industries that she has undertaken leads to further short-term increases in her food deficit, and this is one of the dilemmas presently facing her.

For developing countries generally, overt urban unemployment and rural under-employment, whether open or disguised, are consequences of population growth. The need to deal with overt unemployment presents a clearer choice than that involved in disguised rural unemployment, where economic and non-economic considerations may conflict. Under the extended family system, many persons whose marginal product on the land is lower than their subsistence requirement are sustained because the family shares out the total output among its members. This means that, at a given level of natural resources and their use, a subsistence economy can carry a larger population than a wage economy, for while in the latter many persons would have been unemployed and starved, in the family system they are sustained, by a kind of social security coverage provided by the family. The further argument that this disguised unemployment backlog is potential capital, a hidden resource for expanding production, is not valid unless those concerned are employed elsewhere, at more productive work in accordance with the general principle, considered earlier, which requires the transfer of any factor, labour included, from less to more productive work, and in that manner increasing benefits in relation to costs. But it is economic development and growth which would provide more productive employment and we must thus face again the welfare dilemma, for the movement from a subsistence to a money and wage economy, and hence the dismantling of a built-in and wise social security system, are, to varying degrees, the pre-condition for economic development and growth. In addition, such a development also adds to the total population pressure. The country concerned now has to deal with both the net rate of population expansion and the large mass of individuals who constitute the rural exodus, who leave the shelter of the family in search of employment. Thus a fourth conclusion is suggested, that the low-income countries, in the interest of their development and growth, need to elaborate a policy with regard to their population trends and also relate such a policy to their policy with regard to employment.

The pressure of population on production, levels of income, and consumption, influences international trade, which for low-income countries is a decisive element in their development and growth. There are various imbalances which characterize international trade today. The rich one-third countries of the world account for 80 per cent of the trade, with the poor two-thirds responsible for the remaining 20 per cent. This places the latter in a relatively weak bargaining position. It has been earlier noted that, while manufacturing industry has been growing at the rate of 3.4 per cent, the agricultural sector registered during that period a growth of only 1.4 per cent. This is one simple, if somewhat dramatic, indicator of the falling relative demand for primary products. The interrelated causes which explain this decline include the results of technological progress which lead increasingly to substitution of synthetics, a reduced ratio of raw material components in manufactures, and the curious stabilization in the demand for food-stuffs and other staples, despite the rise in population and incomes, in the industrial countries. A further imbalance is to be found in the fact that while the exports of the manufacturing sector during this period increased by 3 per cent, primary exports expanded by only 1 per cent. This fall in agricultural exports is in part due to their declining production and in part to the considerable expansion of primary production in industrial countries and to action they have taken involving restrictive measures on primary imports, their system of subsidies and surplus disposal. The technological revolution of recent times has taken a long time to reach the primary sector, but starting with the United States and Canada, it has now reached out to all countries of Europe, resulting in the somewhat astonishing phenomena now noted in Europe: the building up of large agricultural surpluses.

It is not surprising, therefore, that the share of the developing countries in the falling rate of primary exports should continue to diminish both absolutely and relatively. During the last ten years there has been some recovery in primary production, and notably in world exports of primary products. While the thirty-year average increase is 1 per cent, for the last ten years world primary product exports have increased at the rate of 4.6 per cent per annum. But even this satisfactory development only increased the imbalance between the developed and developing countries. When examining such statistics, it must be borne in mind that, although developing countries have been largely equated with primary exporters, such an equation is not strictly applicable. Some of the considerations advanced in this analysis apply equally to Australia, New Zealand, and Denmark, which are heavy primary exporters, although not low-income countries. India, for example, like certain other developing countries, also constitutes a somewhat special problem, because its export trade is only partially in primary products, and the ratio of such trade to its gross domestic product is much lower than the average for low-income countries generally. Allowing for these refinements, the improvement in world exports of primary products registered during the last decade constituted a further worsening element for the developing countries. While world exports expanded at the annual rate of 4.6 per cent, for the double reasons just referred to, the primary exports of the developing countries increased only at the rate of 1.9 per cent.[7]

It is at this point that the relative prices of primary and secondary commodities need to be incorporated in the analysis. For the decade 1950–60, prices of primary commodities declined to 94, while the prices of manufactures rose to 126, so that the relative price of agriculture to manufactures was 76. This increase in prices of manufactures is traceable to the increasing demand for manufactures in the high-income countries, with their rising income structure and the expanding demand for manufactures in the low-income countries, resulting from their programme of economic diversification and industrialization at varying levels and in many forms. The results are that during the past decade, the terms of trade of primary commodities fell by over 25 per cent in relation

[7]Raul Prebisch, "Towards a New Trade Policy for Development: Report by the Secretary-General of the Conference" in United Nations, *Proceedings of the United Nations Conference on Trade and Development, Geneva, 23 March–16 June 1964, Vol. II Policy Statements* (E/CONF.46/141, vol. II) (Geneva: United Nations, 1964), pp. 7–13.

to the prices of secondary exports. Some of the developing countries have recently become able to produce and export manufactures, but these efforts to diversify their exports have been frustrated by tariff and non-tariff barriers in the developed countries. Taking into account that, in spite of this situation, some of the developing countries also import primary products and export manufactures and finished goods (e.g., India, Hong Kong, etc.) and taking further into account the fact that this deterioration affected all primary exporters, including the high-income countries such as Australia, New Zealand, and Denmark, the deterioration in the terms of trade for the developing countries must be set at a little over 15 per cent. While primary commodity exports are expanding relatively slowly, the demand for manufactures is rising and will continue to rise rapidly, as a function of development. In addition, account must be taken of the shipping and insurance payments made by the developing countries to the developed countries which carry their trade. In terms of absolute magnitude, the trade gap between the rich and the poor countries is likely, if present trends continue uncorrected, to reach 20 billion dollars by 1970—a date which is all too near. The dimensions of the problem may be realized, if it is noted that current export earnings of all developing countries taken together amount to 20 billion dollars. This imbalance constitutes a serious external bottleneck to development and, unless remedied urgently, will force an even lower rate of growth for the low-income countries than their existing low rates.[8]

This leads to our fifth conclusion on action to be taken at the national and international levels, in the matter of international trade. The constraints for national action in the case of the low-income countries in light of the trade analysis are set forth in three of our previous conclusions. They include: mobilizing all sources of savings, including those resulting from deconcentration of incomes; increasing the productivity of the primary sector, through such measures as reform of the system of land tenure, which is at present a frustrating obstacle to development; and formulating a population policy based on all efforts that will expand the domestic market and enable secondary and tertiary industrial development to

[8]*Ibid.*, pp. 9–13, 55, 56.

play its dynamic role in raising the levels of employment and income. This would include an intensive programme for development of national production structures that can appropriately act as substitutes for imports. The countries must expand and diversify their exports so as to export items for which the world demand is increasing, such as manufactures and semi-finished products. A further related domestic action is the planned development of human resources in all sectors, together with the elaboration of a strategy for development which has been earlier called planning. But there is also action incumbent on the developed countries, action which must be taken in concert with the developing countries, along lines so clearly laid down by the recent United Nations Conference on Trade and Development held in Geneva, in the early months of 1964.[9] These measures include establishment of import targets for primary commodities and industrial goods, a preferential tariff system open to all developing countries, including such action as the Kennedy round of negotiations now underway in GATT, commodity agreements aimed at establishing minimum prices or improvement of prices of primary commodities in relation to the price of manufactures; and a system of compensatory financing to make up for unavoidable deterioration of the terms of trade. Further measures include the readjustment of the external debt, especially for those countries near the take-off point, which are facing a critical situation from the burden of external debt servicing, together with various payment agreements. If these various measures were related to the economic development plan of the low-income countries, they would constitute one significant means of breaking through the interrelated vicious circle which envelops the welfare or rather ill-fare of the developing two-thirds of our world.

The economic development plan of a low-income country must conform to the model discussed earlier, for in suggesting targets and proposing means of achieving them, two basic principles must be followed. The allocation of resources between their different competing uses in the economy of the developing country should be such that no small transfers from one use to another will increase

[9]United Nations, *Final Act of the United Nations Conference on Trade and Development* (E/CONF.46/L.28, June 16, 1964) (Geneva, 1964).

total production and improve distribution. This may seem tautological and the principle may seem obvious that progress must be made on all fronts, at the same time, but no other principle is so often violated and so easily ignored, as a result of various pressures facing the developing country. Planning for an industry or for an occupation must involve the use of resources only up to that point, after which any small transfer elsewhere will not mean a movement to a more preferred position. The second principle, which was only touched upon, is that the interlocking vicious circle of low income, low savings, low productivity (in some cases population pressure), and back again to low income, calls for a comprehensive attack on all fronts, a large movement of resources and a considerable alteration in the structure of the economy and society.

The choices facing a country in the many variables analysed, consumption and investment, primary and secondary production, private and public sectors, the domestic market and the foreign market, are not only alternatives, but are also interrelated quantities, so that in some form or other, for all developing countries, whatever their stage of under-development, planning has to be comprehensive and integral. For each such country, planning will have to deal with a critical minimum mass, which will vary with such elements as the extent of the subsistence sector, the population pressure, the ratio of export earnings to gross domestic product, the current rate and size of development, etc. For some countries, this would mean that the plan must make a concerted drive on all sectors. For others it may involve one major part of the economy, notably the indivisible and interrelated public sector, including both public utilities and social overheads. In still other cases, it may call for a special and marked push forward in certain key sectors, which is one form in which a balanced long-term growth may be assured by a short-term unbalanced growth. This planning of the key variables may mean moving forward in spurts in those industries which are large consumers of the products of other industries or which sell the major part of their output to other industries or both. Finally, for most countries, the planning strategy will call for linking the overall rate of growth with the rate of growth of the slowest moving sector—primary production—because in the end it is the emergence of a minimum marketable surplus in this sector which is the sound foundation for overall growth and development in any economy.

The sixth conclusion which emerges is this: the imperative of comprehensive and integral planning for developing countries. The implementation of development plans calls for use of appropriate techniques relating to public expenditure and public capital formation, which in turn involve sectoral and departmental examination of objectives, priorities and budgets, as tested by the well-worn canons of cost accounting and economic consistency. The other, and in some ways more important, factor which is decisive in the realization and operation of plans is the human resources potential. This is low in all developing countries and involves relative lacks in some key sectors, constituting for many of them the internal bottleneck to development.

The relation between investment and increasing productivity has been dealt with at some length, although in a context which may have seemed to refer only to material investment. The methods employed in computing optimum investment and the relations between rates of growth and savings and investment may have given rise to the same impression. Such was not my intention. The crucial importance of investment in human resources implicit in this analysis now needs further elaboration. The realization that investment in man (of which education is the decisive sector) is of cardinal significance to economic growth has come about through a variety of causes.[10] The importance given to education in Socialist countries is reflected in the writings of Soviet and other Socialist economists,[11] who have computed the returns to a given investment in education at various levels. Inter-country comparisons relating

[10]For further elaboration, see: Malcolm S. Adiseshiah, "Education and Development" in *Restless Nations: A Study of World Tensions and Development* (Council on World Tensions, New York: Dodd, Mead and Co., 1962), pp. 148–62; Malcolm S. Adiseshiah, "Human Resources: Education, Training and Technical Assistance" in *War on Want: Report of a Conference on the United Nations Development Decade held at Christ's College, Cambridge, 13–15 April 1962* (Oxford, London, New York, Paris: Pergamon Press, 1962), pp. 20–61; Frederick Harbison and Charles A. Myers, *Education, Manpower and Economic Growth: Strategies of Human Resource Development* (New York, Toronto, London: McGraw-Hill Book Co., 1964).

[11]Stanislav Strumilin, "The Economics of Education in the USSR," UNESCO, *International Social Science Journal*, vol. XIV, no. 4 (1962), pp. 633–46.

school enrolment ratios and national and per capita income, showing a positive relationship, are being successfully applied to models being built in developing countries, because these correlations are between countries at various levels and stages of development. Intertemporal correlations between education and national income, undertaken for a period of fifty years of the input and output history of one country, show not only that from the consumption side, the income elasticity of demand for education is 3.5, but also that the returns to educational investment, because of its long gestation period, must be sought over a very long period of time.[12] Interindustry correlations have been made to identify the contributions of the education inputs to the total outputs of the firms involved. Further the residual approach,[13] identifying various relationships over time (some fifty years) between labour and capital inputs and total outputs, results in the finding that something between 80 to 90 per cent of the total product are not accountable in terms of labour and capital. All these approaches to the double question of the optimum investment in education and the returns to that investment are still in the early stages of enquiry. As the tools become more refined and the presently inseparable quantities become separable, more exact guidance to the two questions will become available. The main elements in any enquiry into investment in education, stated in somewhat brutal terms here, lead to one general conclusion: that educational investment pays off and that it is a key contributor to growth.

We must thus recognize that the state of technical knowledge and institutional conditions generally cannot be taken as given or as exogenous in the developing countries, but need to be incorporated

[12]Theodore W. Schultz, "Education and Economic Growth," chap. III in *Social Forces Influencing American Education: The Sixtieth Yearbook of Education*, part II (Chicago: The National Society for the Study of Education; University of Chicago Press, 1961), pp. 58–61.

[13]For further discussion of the returns to investment in education and the "residual factor," see: Edward Fulton Denison, *The Sources of Economic Growth in the United States and the Alternatives Before Us* (New York: Committee for Economic Development, 1962); John W. Kendrick (assisted by Maude R. Pech), *Productivity Trends in the United States: A Study by the National Bureau of Economic Research, New York* (Princeton, N.J.: Princeton University Press, 1961); Robert M. Solow, "Technical Change and the Aggregate Production Function," *Review of Economics and Statistics*, vol. XXXIX, no. 3 (Aug., 1957), pp. 312–20; John Vaizey, *The Economics of Education* (New York: The Free Press of Glencoe Inc., 1962).

in the corpus of analysis and conclusions on the economics of development and welfare. The basic issue in this regard is education, which serves several purposes and may be considered both as a productive factor, increasing the productivity of the other agents of production, and as a consumption factor, forming an essential element of the nine components of the levels of living. These consumption and production aspects of education are simultaneously complementary and competitive. They are complementary in the sense that all education is satisfying and all education increases productivity in some measure. They are competitive in the sense that, for poor countries, both in terms of priorities as between the different levels of the educational pyramid, and of educational content as between its humanistic and technical purport, the production function of education receives more attention for the present and will for the duration of their poverty. For the richer countries, on the other hand, both the level and content of education reflect a relative emphasis in its consumption aspects. This double aspect of education which, like the joint production embodied in the banana tree, desired for its fruit and/or its pulp and leaves, makes precise computations as to investment optimum and investment returns in the case of education a long drawn-out and complex process. But using for the demand side a manpower budget approach, and for the supply side the double aspects referred to, and taking into account all other institutional and demand factors in relation to resources, it is possible to plan education towards stated economic and social objectives, as an integral part of a national economic development plan.[14] And so emerges our seventh proposition, that when this integration of the educational sectoral plan in the national plan is assured, the basis is laid for breaking out of the interlocking vicious circle that characterizes the economies of the developing countries, and their pathway to self-sustaining growth is assured.

This path to self-sustaining growth of the developing countries has, except in relation to the analysis and conclusions on international trade (which by its very terms could not be so confined), so far been looked at from the point of view of what these countries can themselves do. But this path is illumined today by a beacon

[14]For detailed discussion of considerations involved in educational planning, see *Economic and Social Aspects of Educational Planning* (Paris: UNESCO, 1964).

light of comparatively recent origin—the beacon light of international co-operation. The main bottleneck to development and growth of the low-income countries has been, as we have seen, shortage of physical and human capital, and it is in this area that the most remarkable evidence of international co-operation is to be seen. Its history is a very recent one. Two decades ago, the suggestion that for purposes of promoting development there might be a transfer of public funds from one country to another would have been regarded as startling, to say the least. In fact, in the nineteenth century, much of the international flow of capital was either for normal investment in industry and agriculture, largely directed to Canada, the United States, continental Europe, and Australia, or for investment in railways, largely directed to India, Argentina, and China. At its height the low-income countries of today received less than 50 million dollars per annum, even as late as the decade before World War I. On the other hand, something up to 30 to 40 per cent of the funds collected by commercial banks in the various colonies of Asia and Africa were remitted, for reasons of profitability and security, to their metropolitan head-offices in Europe during this period.[15] Today, however, public funds for economic development are transferred from the developed to the under-developed countries at the rate of 5 to 6 billion dollars per annum, from Western Europe, North America, Australasia, and Japan. This aid has been growing steadily at the rate of 15 per cent per annum.

In addition, economic aid from the USSR, Eastern Europe, and China, to the developing countries, amounts to around 1,000 million dollars a year, at present. This aid began in a substantial way only in 1954, and information on it is patently incomplete. Most of the aid is in the form of credit and loans, rather than grants. One result of this is that it acts as a means of expanding the area of trade between the developing countries and the socialist countries. This trade expansion, however, does not help to meet the external payment deficits faced by the low-income countries, except in so far as it decreases to some extent imports from the other developed

[15]Edward Nevin, *Capital Funds in Underdeveloped Countries: The Rôle of Financial Institutions* (London: Macmillan; New York: St. Martin's Press, 1961), p. 51.

countries. The relatively small size of the aid total from the socialist countries is to some extent compensated by the fact that its impact on development in the low-income countries is enhanced in two ways: first, this aid is distributed only to a limited number of low-income countries, some 30 out of a possible 120 countries and territories; and second, in most cases this aid is aimed at expanding the investment goods industries of the developing countries, with closely related massive manpower training programmes.

The significance of the inter-country transfer of public funds is great. During the decade 1950–60, the developing countries lost some 17,000 million dollars in export earnings due to the deterioration of the terms of trade. This loss constituted 3/5 of the total foreign aid they received. Aid also constitutes nearly 1/3 of the annual net investment in the developing countries. As their net per capita growth rate is around 2 per cent, this flow is contributing to about half of this net growth rate. It is in this perspective that the United Nations target, calling on all developed countries to earmark 1 per cent of their national income for aid and investment in the low-income countries, must be viewed. Leaving aside the complexities of what constitutes aid, which is a rather murky subject, ranging from straight gifts to short-term credits at 6 to 7 per cent interest rates and occasional high-priced exports, the stakes involved in these financial flows for the world of welfare are high. The earmarking of 1 per cent of their national incomes by the rich countries for aiding the poor ones can be looked at from the side of supply as well as demand. From the supply side, it involves hard choices and sacrifices for the rich countries and their peoples, because the benefits accruing from the opening up of the vast potential markets which the developing countries could provide represent a relatively distant return to current aid. At the present growth rate of the rich countries, which averages around 4 per cent, the allocation of 1 per cent of their national incomes for international aid will involve a sacrifice equivalent to about three months of their economic growth. It may be graphically described, as has been done, as involving the rich countries reaching, on January 1, A.D. 2000, the position they would otherwise have reached in October, 1999. I admit that this is a rather over-simplified picture, but the over-simplification is mainly on the demand side. Turning to the demand side, this international financial flow will contribute to development in the low-income countries only on the assumption that every dollar of such aid is productively invested, conforms to the optimum criteria elaborated so far, and is related to the absorptive capacity and the existing or early development of the needed human resources of the developing country concerned. International aid in terms of the established target and the demand conditions elaborated will double the investment potential of the developing countries and help to bring about a more than doubling of their living levels. This does point to the fact that, while the varying rates of growth between developing and developed countries are sometimes pointed to as a dramatic symbol of the deepening inequalities of the world economy,[16] they need not necessarily be a cause for alarm. Indeed the situation which these rates reflect could serve in the interest of all by lessening such inequalities, in so far as it provides an adequate basis for the contribution to the growth rate of the developing countries by the developed ones.

In this connection the insistence of the aid-giving agency, whether multilateral or bilateral, that its aid will be granted only for a project of high priority which is an integral part of the development plan of the country and which has multiplier effects on the community, and the detailed justification along these lines provided to international and national legislatures authorizing foreign aid programmes, hide the fact that frequently what a given dose of foreign aid really finances is the rather low level project at the margin of the total volume of national activities. The high priority projects, by their very nature and definition, would be financed and executed with national resources, whether or not there was international assistance, if necessary through the purchase abroad of goods and services not available in the recipient country. It is a humbling thought that what foreign aid really helps in many cases are the marginal programmes and projects and it is these which need considerable help and scrutiny. It is the productivity of the

[16]United Nations computations indicate that, given the present rate of population growth, 80 years would be required by the developing countries to attain the average per capita income level of Western Europe, and 120 years to reach the level of the United States, at the present 5 per cent annual growth rate set by the Development Decade. For the lowest income countries, which comprise over one-half of the population of the developing areas, it would require over 200 years to reach the Western European level. (E/Conf.46/141, vol. II, p. 6).

totality of the investment in the country from all sources that is called for, that needs to be assured, and that in its turn assures growth and development.

And so our eighth and final conclusion emerges: everything that can help to bring to a head this movement of international co-operation, both those factors analysed here under aid and earlier under trade, needs urgent attention and active support. The emergence of the concept of soft loans—low interest rate loans with long repayment timings, and initial built-in moratorium periods—is one such significant factor. Again the perspectives opened up by tied loans and grants, if related to balance of payment movements and the era of rapid technological changes in which we are living, can be a contributory force. It was noted earlier that 80 per cent of current international trade and its earnings are shared out between the developed, industrial countries. This means that at no point in time is it mathematically or practically possible for all the rich countries to be facing a balance of payment deficit simultaneously. The problem of balance of payment surpluses and deficits as between the rich countries is on all fours with the problem of my transferring a handful of loose change from one pocket to the other of the jacket I am wearing. Unfortunately, the fiscal and tariff policies of the developed countries seem to have been established for historical reasons, however, on the assumption that each of them and all of them together are facing an external payment deficit at the same time. If the "tieing" of loans and aid can in some simple way be related to those countries which face a deficit, while all others untie their grants, tied loans and aid can become a positive force promoting development. In such a situation, in using not only the primary production surpluses, but also the highly sophisticated capital goods now so quickly classed as technologically obsolescent in our fast-moving world, tied loans and grants will lose a good deal of their emotive force and become tools for development.

And so I conclude. In our micro-economic propositions we moved from consideration of the individual to consideration of the group and the community. In our macro-economic conclusions we have been preoccupied by the ill-fare of nations and a new quantity which we have injected—the needs and constraints of world society, now only beginning to come into focus and whose depth, scope, and unity we merely glimpse today. In this society of nations and world society, our double desiderata, in which have been combined the values of material well-being and freedom, have been to point, on the one hand, to the urgency and necessity of removing limitations on resources and of creating new ones; on the other hand, and partly in consequence, it has been to set in motion a process of continually widening the areas of choice open to man. It is in this context that the platitudinous characterization of our times as one of poverty in the midst of a world of plenty takes on serious welfare overtones. And this in turn brings us back from consideration of the welfare of nations and world society to our starting point— the touchstone of all our propositions and conclusions—the welfare of man.

Growth and development, as the framework of economic action, the motive force of much of macro-economic analysis, are grounded in the welfare of man. Growth rates and development actions considered here are within the welfare framework of the particular societies and cultures in which men and women live, whether they be the Hindu society with its ideal of limitation of want, the Moslem society with its noble egalitarianism, the Buddhist society with its ethical realism, the African tribal society with its realistic simplicity, or the typical Latin American community with its characteristic fluidity, grounded in Christian values. It involves, therefore, no damning of the cow, no shooting of the monkey or the recalcitrant peasant, nor equally no preservation of primitive tribes in their isolated anthropological splendour, no safeguarding of the sanctity of the subsistence sector, to help the economist and the sociologist give his tools the fine edge they presently lack. To me, all economic action is welfare action, because it is grounded in welfare and is both the test and flowering of welfare.

REFERENCES

ALEXANDER KIRKLAND CAIRNCROSS, *Factors in Economic Development* (New York: Praeger, 1962; London: George Allen and Unwin, 1962).

SIMON KUZNETS, *Population, Income and Capital* (International Economics Association, 1955).

PAUL LAMARTINE YATES, *Forty Years of Foreign Trade: A Statistical Handbook with Special Reference to Primary Products and Under-Developed Countries* (New York. Macmillan, 1959; London: Allen & Unwin, 1959).

ORGANIZATION FOR ECONOMIC CO-OPERATION AND DEVELOPMENT, The Mediterranean Regional Project, *Planning Education for Economic and Social Development*, Lectures presented at the training course for Human Resource Strategists organized by the Directorate for Scientific Affairs, Frascati, Italy, (Sept. 3–28, 1962) (OECD, 1963).

P. N. ROSENSTEIN-RODAN, *Notes on the Theory of the "Big Push"* (Cambridge: Mass. Inst. of Technology, Center for International Studies, 1957).

WALT WHITMAN ROSTOW, "The Take-off into Sustained Growth," *The Economic Journal*, vol. LXVI, no. 261, (March, 1956), pp. 25–48.

HANS W. SINGER, "International Aid for Economic Development: Problems and Tendencies," *International Development Review*, vol. VI, no. 1 (March, 1964), pp. 16–21.

UNITED NATIONS, Department of Economic and Social Affairs, *International Economic Assistance to the Less Developed Countries: Report to the Economic and Social Council* (E/3395/rev.1) (New York: U.N., 1961).

UNITED NATIONS, Department of Economic and Social Affairs, *World Economic Survey*, issues for 1960 through 1963.

UNITED NATIONS, Statistical Office, Department of Economic and Social Affairs, *Demographic Yearbook*, issues for 1958 through 1960.

APPENDIX

Agricultural Production in Relation to the Gross Domestic Product at Current Factor Cost* 1961–62

Country	Year	Currency	Total gross domestic product	Agriculture, forestry, hunting, etc.	%
Argentina[a]	1962	Million pesos	1,031,760	218,390	21.2
Australia[b]	1961	Million A pounds	6,526	820	12.6
Austria	1961	Thousand million schillings	152.9	18.1	11.8
Barbados	1962	Million B.W.I. dollars	122.6[c]	34.9	28.5
Belgium	1962	Thousand million francs	560.2	37.4	6.7
Brazil[d]	1960	Thousand million cruzeiros	1,901.2	536.0	28.2
British Guiana	1960	Million B.W.I. dollars	242.9	61.8	25.4
Bulgaria[e]	1961	Million new leva	1,259.8	403.9	32.1
Burma[f]	1962	Million kyats	6,532	6,795	42.8
Canada	1962	Million dollars	35,931	2,482	6.9
Ceylon	1962	Million rupees	6,403.5	2,980.4	46.5
Chile[d]	1962	Million escudos	5,393	527	9.8
China (Taiwan)	1962	Million N.T. dollars	63,129	18,316	29.0
Colombia	1961	Million pesos	28,306	9,526	33.7
Costa Rica	1962	Million colones	2,859.7	954.1	33.4
Cyprus	1962	Million pounds	89.4	21.0	23.5
Czechoslovakia[e]	1962	Million koronas	44,263	6,694	15.1
[g]	1962		____		12.0
Denmark	1962	Million kroner	50,027	6,501	13.0
Ecuador	1962	Million sucres	14,753	5,495	37.2
El Salvador	1962	Million colones	1,579	553	35.0
Fed. of Malaya[h]	1951	Million Malayan dollars	5,495	2,070	37.7
Finland	1952	Million markkas	15,091	2,970	19.7
France	1962	Thousand million francs	353.5[i]	32.5	9.2
Eastern Germany[g]	1962	Million D.M.	79,547	8,150	10.2
Germany, Fed. Rep.	1962	Thousand million D.M.	355.5	18.6	5.2

*A valuation approximating marginal cost to the producer, as opposed to "market prices" which represent a valuation approximating marginal utility to the buyer.

APPENDIX (Continued)

Country	Year	Currency	Gross domestic product at current factor cost		
			Total gross domestic product	Agriculture, forestry, hunting, etc.	%
Greece	1962	Million drachmas	99,766	28,504	28.6
Guatemala	1962	Million quetzales	710.4	246.9	34.8
Honduras	1962	Million lempiras	787.5	351.3	44.6
Hungary[g]	1962	Million forints	155,209	32,236	20.8
Iceland[j]	1962	Million kronur	2,857	501	17.5
India[dk]	1962	Thousand million rupees	154.8	69.7	45.0
Ireland	1962	Million pounds	646	151	23.4
Israel	1962	Million Israeli pounds	5,042	508	10.1
Italy	1961	Thousand million lire	21,589	3,659	16.9
Jamaica	1961	Million pounds	244.3	31.0	12.7
Japan[d]	1962	Thousand million yen	15,499.5	2,201.2	14.2
Kenya	1962	Million pounds	243.3	102.8	42.3
Korea, Rep. of	1962	Thousand million won	252.32	93.10	36.9
Luxembourg	1961	Million francs	23,758	1,794	7.6
Malta	1962	Million pounds	43.5	3.3	7.6
Mauritius	1962	Million rupees	729	192	26.3
Mexico[l]	1962	Million pesos	80,742	15,175	18.8
Morocco[m]	1962	Thousand million dirhams	8.70	2.80	32.2
Netherlands	1962	Million guilders	42,830	3,860	9.0
Nicaragua[n]	1962	Million cordobas	2,911	1,108	38.1
Norway	1962	Million kroner	34,205	3,258	9.5
Pakistan[db]	1961	Thousand million rupees	32.7	17.6	53.8
Panama	1962	Million balboas	470.1	113.9	24.2
Paraguay	1961	Million guaranies	28,746	11,028	38.4
Philippines[o]	1962	Million pesos	12,862	4,246	33.0
Poland[j]	1962	Thousand million zlotys	420.5	93.6	22.3
Portugal	1962	Million escudos	71,933	17,530	24.4
Puerto Rico[b]	1962	Million U.S. dollars	2,029.2	225.8	11.1
Rhodesia & Nyasaland (Fed.)	1962	Million pounds	536.8	116.8	21.8

Country	Year	Currency	Gross domestic product at current factor cost		
			Total gross domestic product	Agriculture, forestry hunting, etc.	%
Rumania[o]	1962			—	29.4
South Africa[d,b]	1962	Million rand	5,481	568	10.4
Spain	1960	Thousand million pesetas	571.3	152.7	26.7
Sudan[b]	1961	Million Sudanese pounds	395.5	232.5	58.8
Sweden[j]	1962	Million kroner	16,733	653	3.9
Syria[q]	1962	Million Syrian pounds	2,987	1,217	40.7
Tanganyika	1962	Million pounds	203.3	117.7	57.9
Thailand	1962	Million baht	63,158[r]	22,216	35.2
Trinidad & Tobago	1962	Million W.I. dollars	1,005.7	103.9	10.3
Turkey	1962	Million Turkish liras	55,829	22,402	40.1
Uganda	1962	Million pounds	155.1	95.0	61.3
U.S.S.R.[g]	1962				22.3
		Thousand million roubles	40.2[t]	6.4	15.9
United Kingdom	1962	Million pounds	24,580	958	3.9
United States of America[d]	1962	Million dollars	447,124	18,267	4.1
Venezuela[u]	1962	Million bolivares	28,585	1,979	6.9
Yugoslavia[v]	1962	Thousand million dinars	3,777	1,046	27.7
[h]	1962	Thousand million dinars	3,475	981	28.2

[a] Not including forestry.
[b] Fiscal year beginning July 1.
[c] Including sugar milling.
[d] Net domestic product.
[e] Gross fixed capital formation.
[f] Fiscal year ending Sept. 30.
[g] Net material product.
[h] At factor cost of 1960.
[i] Not including fishing.
[j] Fixed capital formation.
[k] Fiscal year beginning April 1.

[l] At market prices of 1950.
[m] At market prices of 1960.
[n] At factor cost of 1958.
[o] Net national product.
[p] Net domestic material product at prices of 1961.
[q] Net domestic product at factor cost of 1956.
[r] Hunting, trapping and game propagation are not included.
[s] Gross fixed capital formation at prices of July 1, 1955.
[t] Agriculture and forestry.
[u] At market prices of 1957.
[v] Gross material product.

CHARLES FRANKEL

The Moral Framework of the Idea of Welfare

The Transformation of Welfare

CHARLES FRANKEL

Professor of Philosophy,
Columbia University

Professor Frankel graduated in 1937 from Columbia University with honours in English and Philosophy, took his Ph.D. in Philosophy at Columbia in 1946, after a period of war service in the United States Navy. He has held a Guggenheim Fellowship, a Fulbright (Research) Professorship at the Sorbonne, and a Donnellan Lectureship at Trinity College, Dublin. He has also served as Assistant Secretary of State for Educational and Cultural Affairs in Washington, D.C. Since 1961 Professor Frankel has been engaged in a study of democratic ideas and institutions in societies undergoing rapid modernization. He has published a number of important works, the latest being
The Democratic Prospect, and in 1959 appeared in his own television series "The World of Ideas."

The Moral Framework of the Idea of Welfare

THE LECTURES THAT PRECEDE MINE in this series are at once heartening and disheartening to me. My distinguished predecessors have interpreted their terms of reference so broadly and philosophically that I am encouraged to think that a man whose professional field is philosophy will not be an intruder. But my predecessors have done their work so well that they have also made me wonder just a little what there is left for me to do. Nevertheless, it would be surprising if anyone schooled in the ancient discipline of philosophy should ever find himself quite without words. And it seems to me that, as a philosopher, there may still be a task for me to perform. For welfare is an appealing ideal, a much celebrated one these days, and, in this audience, probably an almost unanimously accepted one. It represents, indeed, the special contribution of our era to the history of human social ideals. Yet it seems to me reasonable and necessary to ask some hard questions about it.

For it is an old habit of mankind to wish to think that everything good is harmonious with everything else that is good, and that a new ideal, if it is compelling in its own terms, will fit naturally and easily with all other ideals that are decent and worthwhile. That we should have to choose between good things—that adding an additional course to our moral menu may require that the whole menu be replanned—this is a disagreeable thought. Yet it may be that the concept of welfare cannot be made to lie down peacefully and easily with traditional ideals and theories of liberal democracy. The thought is at least worth exploring that if we adopt the ideal of welfare, much that we have taken for granted as characteristic and desirable in liberal democratic civilization will have to be recast or perhaps discarded. To understand the concept of welfare, to know what we are doing if we commit ourselves to it, we must ask what its implications are, what changes it makes in the world, and what changes it implies for our way of thinking about the world. And it is as well to begin by asking what its relation is to ideas and ideals that we have long taken for granted.

Certainly there can be no question that the ideal of welfare has already forced us to modify many ideas that our fathers thought to be merely reflections of God's or Nature's laws. Notions about property rights, about the obligations of the individual family, and about the relation between work and income have had to be drastically modified. The freedom of choice of investors has been circumscribed, and the freedom of choice of managers, workers, and even consumers has been affected. Indeed, what we mean by "freedom" in a democracy has been rendered uncertain both in theory and in practice. In theory, there has emerged a troublesomely broadened conception of "freedom" which identifies it with the protection, education, and enhanced well-being of the individual, and not simply with the absence of restraints upon him; in practice, there has emerged an omnipresent state, and there has taken place an incredible multiplication of bureaus, committees, forms, regulations, and requirements, whose central purpose, if we are correctly informed, is the enrichment of individual life, whatever one may think of their actual effect.

But beyond all this, and perhaps most disturbing of all, the concept of welfare appears to raise the prospect—or spectre—of a state which takes it upon itself to define the good life and to train its citizens in the pursuit of that good life. "Experience should teach us," said Brandeis—and it is worth remembering that he was one of the great contributors to the theory of the welfare state— "experience should teach us to be most on our guard to protect liberty when the Government's purposes are beneficent. . . . The greatest dangers to liberty lurk in insidious encroachment by men of zeal, well-meaning but without understanding."[1] It has been a

[1]Dissenting opinion, Olmstead vs. United States, XXX, 277, U.S. 479 (1927).

characteristic of modern liberal democratic theory to maintain that the moral protection and improvement of the citizenry, except within the very broadest and most obvious limits, is not the business of the State. The steady tendency of liberal opinion has been to remove from public control all matters that seem to involve simply differing conceptions of the good life, whether these be personal dress and deportment, drinking, adult homosexual behaviour, or beliefs about God, freedom, and immortality. Yet, on the other side, liberal opinion has now also moved towards giving governments broader and broader powers to advance human welfare. And, illustrating Brandeis' warning, we have seen in our time, in large parts of the world, that the effort by men of zeal to make over society in the light of a moral vision has ended in the rule of Pecksniffs, Philistines, and fanatics.

Can a liberal democracy, which adopts the ideal of welfare as its own, avoid embarking on the same path? I suspect that this unanswered question may lie at the source of a good many of the attitudes towards the welfare state and the welfare society that mark the present time. It is an unspoken fear of the moral busybody with official powers that may explain the bitterness of the complaints about big government, the snide jokes about social workers, and do-gooders, or the nostalgic comparisons of our own "conformist" age with the storied days of the past when, so we are told, men stood on their own feet and needed no one, and certainly no government, to guide them.

What, then, is the relationship of the idea of welfare to cherished conceptions of the proper role and limitations of a liberal state? Before we can answer this question, we must ask some questions about the meaning to be assigned to the idea of welfare. And first among all these questions is whether the idea of welfare can be defined without invoking large and special moral presuppositions. For if it can be, then the doubts about the welfare state that I have mentioned can be dispelled. Can the concept of welfare be morally neutral, or is it inevitably saturated with value-judgments of the most violently personal sort? Is it embedded in an antecedent moral framework, or is it a notion which requires no special tendentious moral point of view? This question bears on issues of peculiar importance to liberal democratic theory, and it is necessary to try to clarify and resolve them if we wish to move into the future with our fundamental social ideas in reasonably good array. It is to this question that I wish to devote this first lecture.

As is the case with many ideas by which we live and by which we sometimes die—freedom, equality, democracy, and justice are some other examples—it is easier to celebrate the idea of welfare than to say exactly what it means. By and large, however, it is used in three quite definite and discriminable contexts—in social work and social assistance, in economics, and in morals, education, and social philosophy. Let us turn first, to the use of the term in social work and social assistance.

The use of the term "welfare" in this context is quasi-technical, but it is now very common and has become part of ordinary speech. It is illustrated in the sentence, "He was in utter misery and had no place to turn, so there was nothing for him to do but to go on welfare." In this usage, welfare is simply the proper good of paupers, just as victory is the good of soldiers and salvation the good of saints. So conceived, welfare would appear to be as far removed from considerations of well-being and the good life as is possible. If it expresses any special moral bias, the bias would seem to be rudimentary and unobjectionable—nothing more than that a civilized society cannot, and in its own prudent self-defence should not, let any of its members starve.

Indeed, in this usage, the term "welfare" is not only, to all appearances, far removed from any positive ideas about the good life, but it also has a quasi-punitive overtone. Its background is in the English poor-law tradition, in which aid to the indigent was basically conceived as part of labour policy, and had as its intention the ensuring of an adequate labour supply.[2] An object of the poor law was to guarantee that no poor man would ever of his own free choice prefer to be without a job than with one. And this remains a basic consideration behind much contemporary welfare legislation. The concept of "welfare" thus rests, it might appear, not

[2]See Karl de Schweinitz, *England's Road to Social Security* (Philadelphia: University of Pennsylvania Press, 1943).

on an ideal of the good life and the good society but only on considerations of dollars and cents.

And yet this concept, as a moment's reflection indicates, carries a considerably heavier moral bias than is commonly supposed. In the first place, it is clearly tied to the prevailing property-system and to the moral beliefs that surround it. Welfare payments are a form of income; and because they are income that does not represent a reward for work, it is considered morally right and economically necessary that they be held to a level below the income of those who work. But there is a peculiar element of distortion in the way this notion that income should normally reflect work is applied. It is not used to justify the abolition of inheritance or to reduce the incomes of the idle rich to subsistence levels. It is used only to place drastic limits on the help extended to the poor. The concept of "welfare," even in its most reduced and minimal sense, is thus connected to a moral code that places special value not so much on work as on the work of the poor.

Nor is this the only way in which this moral code casts its shadow before it. Phrases like "minimal decency," which describe what welfare programmes are presumed to provide, do not stand for a fixed condition of life definable in wholly physical terms. They are relative terms and have psychological and social components. Citizens of the United States who own automobiles and who have cash incomes as high as two or three thousand dollars a year are still classified as falling below the poverty-line. And this is justifiable because poverty, like wealth, is not an absolute state of affairs, but has to be defined in terms of prevailing needs and expectations. Moreover, a minimal standard of life, as it comes to be defined at any time, is also a function of available resources. Principles defining a fair distribution of these resources must therefore also be introduced into the concept of welfare. Even the minimal concept of welfare thus drags behind it a large baggage of moral presuppositions.

A further consideration in support of this conclusion is suggested by a term with which social workers are familiar—"self-determination." Social assistance is commonly aimed, so it is said, at the emancipation of individuals from their state of dependency.

And the social worker is taught to be "non-judgmental," and to avoid imposing his own moral code on the recipient of his help. The object, according to the more or less official doctrine, is simply to enable the individual eventually to live his own life by depending on his own resources and making his own decisions. But there are few social workers, after all, who would think of themselves as having succeeded in this laudable exercise if the client who was the object of their ministrations, having been brought to a condition of self-determination, self-determinedly went out and became a successful embezzler. The fulfilment of individual potentialities does not really include the fulfilment of any and all kinds of potentiality. The concept of "self-determination," for all its apparent moral neutrality, is a morally loaded term.

Indeed, "self-determination" obviously rests on the prevailing moral judgment that a state of personal independence is greatly to be preferred to a state of dependency. Admirable though this judgment is, it is a *judgment*, not a reading of some pellucid law of nature. There have been civilized societies that would have found such a judgment odious. "Self-determination" was not, for example, the moral ideal that governed feudal lords when they protected and helped their serfs. Welfare in the reduced sense which it has been given in the context of social assistance is a special moral ideal belonging to an era in history in which "dependency" has been regarded as something shameful that ought at all costs to be avoided. Men in the middle ages took it for granted that they depended on their families, guilds, and local communities; they generally regarded going-it-alone as madness, if not criminal disloyalty. They did not have a concept of dependence or of independence as we construe the terms, and the idea of welfare in its modern meaning would have been incomprehensible to them. The resources which modern societies pour into welfare programmes are the tax they pay, in a word, for their commitment to the morality of individualism.

If this analysis has any validity, even the narrowest concept of welfare comes trailing clouds of morality behind it. But the case is even more striking when we turn to the concept of welfare in its second and larger meaning—in its use, that is to say, in the science of economics. Here, as Professor Marshall has already pointed out, welfare is related to wealth rather than only to relief from the sharper forms of suffering. Welfare is what contemporary economic planning takes to be its goal.

The economist's interest in welfare, however, is by no means recent in origin. Welfare has always been a central theme for the economist, albeit an elusive one. Adam Smith was interested not only in the conditions making for an equilibrium of supply and demand, but in ways to enhance the wealth of nations. Ricardo distinguished between the two concerns of economists, one in "value," the other in "riches." "Value" is what a commodity or service commands in the market; it is the economic factor which, under ideal conditions, determines the kinds and quantities of goods and services that are produced, exchanged, and consumed. The concept of "riches," in contrast, is harder to define, but it is what all the work, and all the buying and selling, presumably are for. It is the measure we are looking for when we try to determine whether, as a consequence of a given set of changes in the quantities of goods and services that make up the economic universe, we are really better off.

Now, to be interested in the welfare of a society, to wish to see it richer and better off, obviously cannot mean simply to add to the gross amounts in dollars and cents of the commodities that are produced and exchanged. As we know, money is subject to fluctuations in its value, and so are any other physical objects that we may use to measure value, whether they are diamonds, gold bars, wampum, or eggs. Even more to the point, wealth or riches or welfare have a psychological aspect to them. They have to do with what is satisfying or serviceable to a man, and this is not necessarily the same as their value in the market place. There is no point in giving a starving man on a desert island a diamond stickpin instead of a can of beans, and while both a shovel and a copy of the *Critique of Pure Reason* may sell for seven dollars, they have a different utility to different men.

How, then, do we measure the "welfare" of a society? Is there an impersonal standard available to us when we talk of increasing the wealth of society? This is not the place to examine in detail the attempts that economists have made to formulate such a standard, but enough can be said about them in their general outlines, I believe, to allow us to make a reasoned judgment about the possibility of removing special moral presuppositions from the concept of social welfare.

Broadly speaking, the efforts of economists to develop a value-free, "scientific" concept of welfare have taken two directions. The first has been utilitarian. In this approach, the effort has been made to define the concept of social welfare in terms of the actual preference-curves of individuals. By aggregating these individual preference-curves in some way, it has been hoped, a definite and morally untendentious meaning can be given to the concept of social welfare. Unfortunately for such efforts, however, some staggering ethical preconceptions seem to remain.

One arises from the assumption that the satisfactions or "utilities" of different individuals can actually be compared. I do not deny, of course, that this can be done. We do it, in fact, all the time. Jones, we say, gets more pleasure from television than Smith gets; Peter is as happy with his seventh glass of beer as Paul is listening to his seventh lecture on the concept of welfare. But it is difficult to see just what could be meant by such interpersonal comparisons unless they are made in terms of some standard of comparison; and whose standard shall we use, Jones's or Smith's, Peter's or Paul's? Normally, I suspect, we in fact tacitly employ social norms or standards, believing they are shared—or, perhaps, should be shared—by the individuals concerned. But this is not to develop a value-free standard of social welfare; it is to accept reigning standards or implicitly to suggest others.

Moreover, quite apart from the problem posed by interpersonal comparisons of individual utilities, there is a second preconception in utilitarianism which seems to import a moral premise into the discussion. Paul, who enjoys lectures on the concept of welfare, is obviously more discerning and deserving than Peter, who is content to become bloated with beer. Yet utilitarianism insists that Paul's satisfaction shall count for no more than Peter's. In the effort to avoid ethical judgment, utilitarianism refuses to distinguish between the worth of Peter's satisfactions and Paul's. But it is just as much an ethical judgment to say that the differences in the moral worth of individuals should be ignored in measuring social utility as that they should be taken into account.

Finally, is it good to give people what they want? The construction of a social welfare function out of the empirically determined preference scales of living individuals presupposes that this ethical principle is valid. I am prepared to grant that it is preferable to the general principle that it is wrong to give people what they want. But I am not prepared to agree that there can never be any reasonable argument on the matter.

Nor do we successfully avoid ethical preconceptions, it seems to me, by adopting a second, highly sophisticated approach that has been taken towards the problem. Starting with Pareto, economists have made the attempt to define social welfare without presupposing the comparability of the satisfactions of different individuals. Instead, they have introduced a conception of a "social optimum," defined as that state of affairs in which further improvement is impossible because no individual can move to a position he would prefer without causing some other individual to move to a position he likes less. Working within this framework, it has then been thought possible to develop impersonal, non-moral measures of increments of welfare by determining what compensatory payments or benefits the disadvantaged individual would be willing to accept to allow his position to be made worse. This process of social bargaining would presumably allow us to place a value on proposed additions to the well-being of a set of individuals.

As is apparent, this approach tries manfully to avoid introducing an outside, moral point of view, and attempts instead to build a conception of social welfare out of the actual preference of individuals. I am not competent to pass judgment on its value as a contribution to economic theory and, happily, it is not my function to do so. Economists will be better able to judge both its merits and the significance of the prickly technical problems it involves.[3] So far as I can see, however, it does not succeed in purging "welfare" of moral bias any more than any of the other attempts we have

[3]For a lucid introduction to these issues see the essay by Kenneth Boulding, and the comments by Melvin Reder and Paul Samuelson, in *A Survey of Contemporary Economics*, vol. II, ed. Bernard F. Haley (Homewood, Ill.: Richard D. Irwin, Inc., 1952).

examined. Like utilitarianism, it assumes that it is right to give people what they want. Secondly, it assumes a state of affairs in which every man has his price, and people are willing to trade anything for anything else. This would be, no doubt, a business-man's paradise, but it imposes an artificial and slanted psychology on the real world. Third, and most to the point, it takes it that trade and bargaining are the preferred ways to determine the real worth of things. But how do we establish through bargaining what a man's religion means to him, or his family, or his self-respect? The man who would bargain about any of these, it might be said, does not know what they are. Yet to leave them out of account in giving a meaning to the word "welfare" is to leave out the heart of the matter.

We are beginning to have strong reasons to suspect, then, that it is not possible to cut off the meaning of the word "welfare" con-veniently so that it does not take us into the stormy waters of ethics and philosophy. On the contrary, if what I have said so far has any validity, "welfare" is a term which, though it may not mean exactly the same thing as "virtue" or "social justice," is neverthe-less intimately related to these terms, and cannot be defined without recourse to them. But is it impossible, then, that at this level—at the level at which welfare is related to our conception of the kind of well-being that men and societies ought to seek—we can find some neutral and impersonal way to define welfare? Can ethics or philoso-phy get us off the moral limb, as it were, by providing us with a rational, neutralized conception of welfare that all reasonable men can accept?

On the whole, professional philosophers, in contrast with eco-nomists, lawyers, and sociologists, have paid relatively little direct attention to the concept of welfare as such, treating it, on the whole, only in connection with some of the classic themes of moral philosophy, like "virtue," "the good life," and "justice." Such dis-cussions, and particularly discussions of social justice, have an obvious bearing on our theme, however, for welfare is commonly regarded as an ingredient of, or at any rate something closely related to social justice. And there are some major philosophical analyses of justice which are particularly relevant, for they seem to suggest we might somehow escape the pitfalls of moral disagreement by embedding justice and welfare in some deeper set of necessary truths. The most appealing among such philosophical efforts are those that attempt to show that justice, and presumably welfare, are related to basic human rights, and that universal principles of right reason support a belief in such rights.

I know you will understand that I do not mean to argue against a belief in universal human rights in what I am going to say; still less do I wish to suggest that welfare has no place among these rights. But I am interested in determining what sort of argument is involved in asserting that there are universal human rights and that welfare is among them.

The most obvious problem encountered by the attempt to find a morally neutral basis for human rights involves the well-known difficulty of asserting any moral principle to which reasonable exceptions cannot be found. The only way to avoid this is to state the principle in terms so broad that nothing definite is any longer at issue. "Killing is wrong" becomes "wrongful killing is wrong"; "all children have a right to an education" becomes "all children have a right to an education provided there are no superior social interests for which the resources of the society should be used." This does not mean, to be sure, that such statements, in the contexts in which they are ordinarily used, have no function. Given the aspirations of men today, given the imperatives of modern life, they surely express claims that have a *prima facie* right to our most serious consideration. But in interpreting and applying these statements in specific contexts, they have meaning only in so far as we read meaning into them, and for this, it seems to me, we must bring a larger framework of moral assumptions with us.

Yet the belief in basic human rights is one to which most of us, as it is easy to understand, cling desperately; and given the long-existing traditions of Western thought, it is natural that the demand for some transcendent rational foundation for such a moral belief dies hard. Accordingly, almost throughout the history of philosophy, there have been ingenious attempts to circumvent such elementary arguments as those I have just offered. The revival of such efforts to find a transcendental or absolute foundation for human rights is one of the conspicuous characteristics of the present period in philosophy. One effort that has attracted attention is that of Professor John Rawls, who has argued that basic human rights can be derived from a fundamental concept of justice, and that the validity of this concept can be established, in turn, by morally neutral arguments that should compel the assent of any reasonable man. Although Professor Rawls' argument is focussed on justice rather than on welfare as such, a discussion of his argument will, I think, bring to the surface some of the fundamental problems that attend any effort to take all elements of moral relativity out of key social ideals like justice or welfare.

Let us suppose, says Professor Rawls,[4] that a group of ideally rational men exist who have a mutual self-interest in remaining together. They are rational in the sense that they know their own interests reasonably well; that they are capable of intelligent forethought; that they can stick to a plan of action without being turned aside by momentary impulses or temptations; and, finally, that they are not moved by envy. "The bare knowledge or perception of the difference between their condition and that of others," says Professor Rawls, "is not, within certain limits and in itself, a source of great dissatisfaction."

Now let us further suppose, says Rawls, that one of our rational men had a complaint against the others. As a condition for adjudicating this complaint it would obviously be necessary to agree on the principles to be employed in adjudication. How could this agreement be reached? The most obvious method would be to let everybody make his own suggestions concerning the principles that should be adopted. If any of these suggestions were to have a chance to be accepted, however, certain rules governing the making of suggestions would also have to be introduced. Each man would have to agree that if his suggestions were adopted, everybody's complaints, and not only his own, would be tried on the same principles; he would also have to agree that the principles adopted on any one occasion would remain in force, short of special circum-

[4]See his articles "Justice as Fairness," *Philosophical Review*, LXVII (1958), and "Constitutional Liberty and the Concept of Justice" in *Nomos VI, Justice*, ed. Carl J. Friedrich and John W. Chapman (New York: Atherton Press, 1963).

stances, on all future occasions. Thus, no one would risk partiality, and fairness would be in everybody's interest.

If these reasonable rules of the road were adopted, what rules would all the members of the group think it reasonable to adopt? They would all agree to be governed, Professor Rawls believes, by a fundamental concept of justice. In accordance with this concept, each person who participates in a social institution or who is affected by it would have an equal right to as much liberty as is compatible with an equal liberty for all; secondly, any inequalities in the way in which the institution distributed the benefits and burdens that go with maintaining it would be regarded as arbitrary and unjustifiable unless it could be reasonably expected that such inequalities actually worked out to everybody's advantage; thirdly, everyone would have to have a chance to try for the more favourable positions in a fair and open competition. This concept of justice thus combines three basic principles—liberty, equality, and reward for services contributing to the common good.

Now at first blush, such a concept of justice certainly seems fair enough. It presents justice, indeed, just as elementary fairness, and it would certainly seem as though any reasonable man, no matter what his other moral commitments, would accept this principle. There are, nevertheless, some reasons why I remain not entirely persuaded that we have found a wholly untendentious conception of justice.

The first principle in this conception of justice is that each person participating in a social institution has a right to as much liberty as is compatible with an equal liberty for all. Certainly, it seems natural enough that a group of morally autonomous, rational individuals would choose to adopt such a principle. But this is the rub. The elements of this conclusion have already been presupposed in the conditions for solving the problem. Our imaginary group of rational men consists precisely of free, autonomous individuals, each of whom must speak for himself, and none of whom can speak for anyone else. But why should individuals be the ultimate moral units? Why not families, or clans extending over many generations, or churches, or corporations? To ascribe moral autonomy to biological individuals is in fact the exception rather than the rule if the whole history and spectrum of human moral attitudes is taken into account. Admirable as the ideal of autonomy may be, the dice have been loaded in favour of a special moral point of view when it is automatically accepted as a preliminary to defining and defending a concept of justice.

The second element in the idea of justice, as proposed by Professor Rawls, is that any inequality be rejected as arbitrary unless it is reasonable to suppose that it contributes to everybody's advantage. But what is it that our hypothetical rational men would actually accept when they agreed to this principle? Let us work from the end of the formula back to the beginning. Consider the phrase "to everybody's advantage." How shall we interpret it?

Do we mean everybody's advantage as determined by some independent standard, apart from the subjective preferences of the individuals concerned? We then have the problem of justifying this standard, and of determining on just what grounds the members of the group would give their common consent to its adoption. Or do we mean by "everybody's advantage" what each man thinks is to everybody's advantage? We then have the problem of adjudicating among competing points of view, and are back where we started. Probably, then, we mean by "everyone's advantage" simply what each separate individual thinks is to *his* advantage. This, presumably, is what Professor Rawls has in mind. But here, again, we have a disturbing problem. We have to assume that, where no common standard of mutual advantage is available, there is never any justice unless some bargain can be struck, some balance of incommensurate interests found, which all reasonable men will consider an advantage to themselves. But this is to propose a standard of justice which will be of little use where the most difficult and troublesome social problems are concerned.

In any case, why should we assume that an inequality is unjust unless each individual affected finds it to his net advantage? Are there not some practices which, in appropriate circumstances, we should be prepared to accept as just, even though representative individuals affected could not reasonably regard the inequality as making things better for themselves? Robin Hood's stealing from the rich to give to the poor is a case in point. So is confiscatory taxation, or the policy followed by many developing countries of removing aliens from favoured positions and replacing them with native citizens. Difference of opinion about the justice of these practices is at least conceivable among reasonable men.

As may by now have been suggested, there are analogous difficulties in fixing just what is meant by "inequality." "Equality" and "inequality" are terms to which no definite meaning can be assigned unless the respects in which people are being compared, and the standards of comparison to be employed, are specified. At this point, however, substantive theoretical, practical, or moral judgments have to be made, at least tacitly, that such and such a basis of comparison is significant and important, while another basis of comparison is not. In fact, the most important arguments about inequality usually have little to do with whether a given standard is being fairly applied. They have to do, much more often, with the nature of the standards that are applied, and turn on the proposal that different and better standards be substituted. The formula proposed by Professor Rawls is not capable of solving such questions, but presupposes that they will not arise.

In addition to the difficulties attached to giving meaning to the formula proposed by Professor Rawls unless we make appropriate moral presuppositions, there is also the moral bias present in his definition of "rationality." His rational man, he argues, will not be moved by envy: the perception that others are better off "is not, within certain limits and in itself, a source of great dissatisfaction." But the phrase "within certain limits" is clearly relativistic; what some people and some societies have come to accept as minor inequalities others regard as beyond all decent limits. And beyond this, why is envy "irrational"? From a non-moral point of view, is it not simply one more human interest? If Jones is envious of Smith and if we cut Smith down to Jones's size, will this not make Jones feel better, and will we not, then, have contributed to Jones's advantage? If we bring envy into our calculations, however, it becomes more difficult than ever to accept as intelligible a standard of justice which demands that all inequalities be to everybody's advantage. Yet I see no non-moral grounds for excluding envy. Unless we specify the particular context in which we are making the judgment, envy is an emotion which is no more "rational" or "irrational" than self-interest, mother's love, gregariousness, or the desire for revenge. Nor is this simply an abstract point made for the purposes of debate. Envy, like self-interest, is a powerful and fairly widespread human emotion, and it is present in many of the quarrels between men in which they call for "justice." The government of man depends on dealing with it, not ignoring it. The exclusion of envy from the traits of Professor Rawls' model rational man is undoubtedly a methodological convenience; but it is also, I think, a moral prejudice, and an unrealistic one.

Professor Rawls includes in his concept of justice the idea of positions open to competition by everyone. This idea is also open to objections, since it makes the assumption that a distribution of rewards and burdens is "fair" if it reflects the relative merits of individuals. But individual merit is not the only possible basis for differentiating between individuals in terms of what is due to them. Individual needs are also, in principle, a relevant criterion. In general, Professor Rawls' account of justice appears to ignore the fact that there can be several other criteria for determining the "fair" or "just" distribution of the goods and ills of this world besides service to the common good, and that many of the classic problems of distributive justice are intelligible only if we see that they involve weighing the claims of such different criteria against one another.

Moreover, even if we restrict justice to distribution in accordance with individual merit, we have still to ask how we determine "merit." The rule that competition for all positions be fair and open is hardly sufficient. In the first place, we cannot automatically assume that competition for open positions is always the best and most reasonable way to find out who is the man who serves the common interest best, since the capacity to win or to hold a position is not necessarily the same as the capacity to perform its functions well. And even if we make this favourable assumption, have we said very much until we say something about the actual nature of the rules that govern the competition? Different games yield different victors, and a man who is always the loser in a given game may well complain, not that the game is fought unfairly, but that it is the wrong game, rewarding merits of the wrong kind, and never giving a fellow with his kind of talent a chance. The rules of chess are not favourable to basketball players, and the competition of the marketplace is not competition by rules which are likely to permit poets or philosophers to demonstrate their worth. If I am not mistaken, this is the nature of many kinds of social protest. To decide to have "open competition," then, is not all that is needed to settle questions of justice. Certain choices among kinds of competition have to be made, and this requires, surely, some additional moral premises.

Indeed, my summary objection to the conception of justice Professor Rawls offers is that it is in the main a formalistic and procedural one. It defines justice essentially in terms of ways of making decisions. But justice has not only a procedural but a substantive aspect. When men complain about injustice, they are complaining as often as not about outcomes, not procedures; they are not saying that the rules were applied unfairly, they are saying that the rules are bad rules. And at this level an appeal to a higher order concept of justice which is itself purely procedural would not appear to settle the problem. We are back at one of the standing problems of philosophy—how to derive substantive conclusions from premises that are purely formal or procedural in character. It does not appear to me to be the case that contemporary philosophy has solved this "problem" any better than philosophy in the past; I do not think it can be solved. If we wish to have a concept of justice or of welfare capable of giving us guidance in determinate contexts, we need to give that concept content; and its content will come from the larger moral code which we accept or espouse.

There are many who believe, of course, that only ideals that have a transcendent character, that are discovered rather than chosen by human beings, can provide a sound basis for a free society. In denying this claim of transcendence, I do not mean to say that there is no sound basis for a free society. I mean only to say that without antecedent moral commitments there is no argument for welfare, justice, or a free society, and that these moral commitments cannot be transmuted into anything but what they are—moral commitments. Certainly, they cannot be reduced without remainder simply to promises or contracts or the rules of reasonable men. Indeed, to me, what is really puzzling is why anyone should think that moral ideals acquire somehow a higher moral status when it is shown that they can be derived from principles that are not moral at all.

Welfare, then, is a moral ideal for which we have to take full responsibility. Neither God nor Nature nor Pure Reason nor The Market System will let us off the moral hook. The content we give it is a matter, at least in part, of the content we choose to give it. And there will be implications in our choice. For "welfare" is not a narrow term disconnected from terms like "virtue" or "the good life." To be an advocate of "welfare," or to be the official, citizen, or beneficiary of a "welfare state," is to be implicated in decisions and policies that involve large judgments about the proper ends of life.

But what moral judgments, then, should we accept as the foundations of our concept of welfare? What basis exists for preferring one such moral judgment to another? And if the State, in accepting the responsibility to be concerned about the welfare of its citizens commits itself to tendentious moral views about the nature of everyman's welfare, have we not come to the end of the road so far as liberal ideals of government and politics are concerned?

The Transformation of Welfare

I AM AFRAID THAT THE EXERCISE in philosophical scepticism in which I invited you to join me yesterday may have left you with the sour feeling that philosophy is simply an unjustly honoured way of making mischief. If that is so, you will not be the first in whom philosophy has aroused such feelings; I confess that when I notice the mischief that other philosophers make I often have that feeling too. Still, I have no apology to offer for my scepticism: well-founded doubts are generally to be preferred to ill-founded affirmations, no matter what the partisans of positive thinking may tell you. And apart from this, my scepticism, such as it was, was in my mind only a necessary propaedeutic to the asking of more fundamental questions concerning the meaning that should be assigned to "welfare," the intellectual basis for doing so, and the relation of this concept to established ideals of liberal civilization. It is to these matters that I shall now turn.

The first question before us, in the light of what has been said, concerns the intellectual basis of any definition of "welfare" that we may offer. If the remarks I made previously were in their main direction justified, then "welfare" is an incurably moral concept, and there is no demonstrative proof that all people must adopt this ideal or must give it one meaning rather than another. At least in part, both the commitment to the ideal of welfare and the specification of its meaning must be matters of choice, matters of moral policy. And this will no doubt have led many of you to believe that, in my view, the adoption and definition of the ideal of welfare are arbitrary and personal affairs, and subject to no form of intellectual control. But while this may just possibly be the logical implication of my position, I do not believe that that is the case.

The absence of a transcendental basis for certifying moral judgments does mean that the moral values to which we happen to be committed are not deducible from universally valid premises, and are therefore, in a purely technical and wholly harmless sense of the word, logically arbitrary. But this does not mean that there is no external basis for examining or criticizing these values. For we are men bound down to specific situations and faced by definite problems, and the values we hold, if they mean anything at all, direct us to define these problems in certain ways and to seek solutions to them that will serve certain ends. But are these problems solvable when so defined? Are the ends sought achievable? And if they are, what is their cost, their impact on other values? Briefly, we may consider our values, I suggest, as guides in the formation of hypotheses for the solution of definite problems. And in relation to their capacity to perform this function, they can be accepted, dismissed, corrected, modified, or expanded. Nor do I think that I describe anything but what we normally do when we make new value-judgments. It is on grounds of this sort, I believe, and not by geometrical reasoning from universal axioms, that most thoughtful men and women in our generation have come to reject, for example, Puritanical ideas of sexual morality or the ideal of absolute laissez faire in the economy. And it seems to me that it is in these terms that we may also develop the notions of welfare that might guide us through our present problems.

From this point of view, then, what is the moral content to be assigned to the idea of welfare? What general meaning can we give to the concept such that it is likely to serve as a fruitful and effective organizing principle for contemporary social policy? We can begin to work our way towards the answer to this question, I think, if we reflect on the context in which the modern idea of welfare emerged, and compare this context with that in which the idea must now function.

I have already remarked on the close historical connection between the concept of welfare still employed in social work and social assistance and the evolution of labour policy in the modern world. This close connection between the concept of welfare and the value placed on labour is not only historical but philosophical. It was part of a guiding hypothesis offered for the reorganization of modern economics and politics, and for the liberation of these from traditional forms of control. The philosophy of John Locke is perhaps the prime illustration.

In Locke's view, it was the labour a man performs, and only that, which gives him his right to external property. Before the invention of money, however, there were natural limitations on how much property any individual could or would accumulate. For since property was perishable and there was therefore no point in striving for possessions beyond one's immediate needs, the danger that one man's accumulation would deprive another man of the chance to acquire property was slim or non-existent. All the world, as Locke put it, was America.

However, once money was invented, accumulation beyond the limits of the individual's immediate needs became possible; and because men consented to the use of money, such accumulation was perfectly just. Thus, for Locke, all inequalities in the possession of property, even those so extreme that they reduce some individuals to the status of paupers, are all in accord with the rules of justice, at any rate in so far as justice is a matter of property rights. Nor are there any considerations of justice, so conceived, that require individuals, as Locke saw it, to come to the help of their fellows, or to provide them with necessities which they had not provided themselves through their own labour.

Yet this does not mean that Locke saw no basis for regulating or limiting accumulation. His entire discussion of property indicates that he recognized that reasonable questions can be asked about any state of affairs in which a man accumulates more than he needs. Governments, in fact, have as one of their functions the regulation of accumulation. "It is plain," says Locke, "that the consent of men have agreed to a disproportionate and unequal possession of the earth, I mean out of the bounds of society and compact." But "in governments the laws regulate it; they having, by consent, found out and agreed in a way how a man may rightfully, and without injury, possess more than he himself can make use of. . . ."[1] Yet such regulations and limitations do not follow from considerations of strict property-right justice. What imposes an obligation on individuals to share some of their surplus with their fellows, what justifies social limitations on the right to accumulate property, is not justice but charity.

If some men have more than they need, and others have less, the poor have a claim to the help of the rich. But this is not because the poor have a property right, and not because, in this special sense, it is just that they should have enough to take care of their needs. It is because God and Reason command us to love our fellows, and because no man has the right to determine, when he can prevent it by his action, that another man shall die. Thus, the rule of charity provided for Locke an ultimate limiting condition beyond which inequalities of accumulation could not be permitted to go. In charity we have a residual concept, a principle we invoke when the normal rules of the system break down. To give a man charity is to give him what he has not earned, through his work, and what is not, therefore, justly his; it is to give recognition to his needs, but a kind of minimal, last-ditch recognition. His needs have a claim on us, as it were, only if he is needy.[2]

The concept of welfare as it functions today in social work and social assistance has of course undergone changes, but its intellectual source, I believe, lies here. Welfare is the child of charity— it is associated with the notion of unearned relief from distress. It is something that cannot be brought within the sphere of the controlling doctrine that work is the sole justification for receiving any benefits from others. Welfare activities, accordingly, have been regarded as essentially exceptional in character; they deal with boundary-line conditions; there is a stigma attached to them; the recipients of welfare, if they are not always beyond the pale, are not quite within the pale either. Seen from the point of view of its seventeenth-century origins, the concept of welfare is what might be called a "waste-basket" concept. It is where we file the problems

---

[1] John Locke, *Treatise on Civil Government*, II, 5, 50–1.

[2] See the article by Raymond Polin, "Justice in Locke's Philosophy" in *Nomos VI, Justice*, ed. Carl J. Friedrich and John W. Chapman (New York: Atherton Press, 1963).

that fall outside strict considerations of property and of justice.

The function which this set of ideas has served will, I think, be plain to you. It helped free Western society from a system of fixed feudal tenure and from habits of thought and feeling bred by a subsistence economy; it helped adjust the Western mind and Western institutions to a new state of affairs in which the progressive expansion of productivity had become a fundamental desideratum. The philosophy that makes individual work central, and that treats as a side issue the provision for basic human needs that cannot be met through individual work, is part of the great movement of Western society that has been described as the movement from status to contract. So conceived, the traditional concept of welfare has played an indispensable historical function. The philosophy to which it belongs helped Western society to understand and to believe in what it was doing when it destroyed the economic power of the manor, the church, and the guild, and shifted from a system of involuntary mutual dependence to one of individual mobility and voluntary contract. Welfare under this new state of affairs took care of functions for which no place could be found in the new pattern of free entrepreneurs, free labourers, and free contracts— functions which had once been performed not as afterthoughts, but in the natural course of events by the family, the church, the manor, and the guild. Implicitly, it prepared a new way of carrying on such functions, and offered the hypothesis that this new way was more likely to yield the greater liberty and greater productivity that were desirable. It was an hypothesis for its own time, and we must ask whether it is still a usable hypothesis in ours.

To begin to answer this question we must notice that the philosophy we have been describing was, in fact, never quite so neat as it seemed. As time went on it was subjected to extensive adjustments; and in these adjustments there can be discerned the slow growth of another idea of welfare—one that has been and remains dim and not fully articulate, but which, in our generation, we may finally be able to seize, to state, and to use. In the first place, despite all that the philosophy we have been describing did to make reward for individual work the basic element in what we mean by justice, recognition of the special claims of kinship and family always remained strong. Inheritance was never abolished. The social system to which the philosophy was applied, and which it presumably explained and justified, was never in its main lines a system of individual motivation for individual gain, but rather of individual motivation for family gain. And on the assumption that families would remain, and could provide effective support to individuals, it could be presumed, without excessive callousness, that public provision for the needs of those who could not themselves meet their needs under a free contract system would be mainly provision for widows, orphans, and vagabonds.

But such a presumption—the presumption that the system of free contract, softened by familial affections and customary decencies, would by itself provide adequately for the normal needs of most normal members of society—could not, of course, be indefinitely maintained. Workers became more loosely tied to the surrounding community. Local economies became national in size, and the necessity for broad agreements and common standards to govern the flow of people, goods, and services became more urgent. Corporate and bureaucratic forms of organization came to replace the more personalistic habits and standards of family capitalism. Production and exchange became steadily more technical, making it more difficult for ordinary intelligent men to depend on their own judgment in drawing up the terms on which they entered the economy, and the accumulation and concentration of capital made it more and more obviously a caricature to describe the relation between the individual worker and his employer as a bargaining relation between equals. And the steady erosion of customary ways of doing things destroyed the inherited regulatory framework for contracts, and forced individuals and society at large to look for new modes of regulation and self-protection. Extensive adjustments in the free-contract system have had to be made, accordingly, and, as time has gone on, they have become increasingly rapid.

To a very considerable extent, these adjustments have been made while using the language and litany of "free contract." The words have remained unchanged; but what they putatively describe has had less and less of a relationship to these words. For the fact is that the development of Western society in the modern era cannot be described unequivocally as a movement from status to contract.

It has also been characterized by another movement, parallel to the first and intimately connected with it, but in the reverse direction. This has been a movement from contract to status. A very large number of the economic and social relationships which we persist in describing as "contractual," and which we unreflectively classify as based on free individual agreements, are contractual in only a very stretched sense of the word. The contract is a disguise; it is a form by which social recognition and protection are given to the legitimate needs of people falling into certain general categories, or occupying certain general positions in society.

Examples abound.[3] Modern marriages are sealed by contracts, but the parties do not bargain over the essential terms, and have no right to do so; a marriage contract falls into a pre-established form defined by law and custom. A married woman cannot win improvements in her legal status by individual negotiation with her spouse, but only by changing the laws. For the fundamental rights and obligations of husbands and wives are matters of legal status, and not of free agreement. The marriage "agreement" consists largely in the mutual performance of a ceremony which subjects the parties to certain laws to which they were not hitherto subject. And beyond this, even where the governing arrangements between individuals are not set by law but by explicit agreement, the agreement is often a far cry from an individual contract. Most of the contracts to which we put our names are in point of fact standard, printed forms.

The gap between language and reality is equally great when we turn to other areas. Modern insurance techniques in effect substitute collective responsibility for individual liability, and the advent of compulsory insurance in many areas of life deprives the individual even of the right to choose individual liability. Perhaps most obvious of all, the major agreements that affect our economy are not free agreements between individuals but products of collective bargaining. The individuals who are bound by these agreements are bound not as individuals but by virtue of their status as members of groups. Probably the greatest change wrought by the American New Deal consisted, indeed, in the recognition of the rights of

[3]See Morris R. Cohen, "The Basis of Contract" in *Law and the Social Order* (New York: Harcourt, Brace, 1933).

groups, and not simply of individuals. And the bargains made
between these groups cannot be accurately described as consequences of the play of a free market. They are in large part
consequences of a contest for power and public approval, or of
guesses about the probable outcome of such contests, and a very
large political element is present in them.

In short, while we have, until recently, been talking in one way
in Western society, we have been acting in a different way more
often, perhaps, than we have realized. Under the rubric of free
contracts, we have developed collective procedures for taking care
of the needs of people in certain types of situation or position.
Whether we take care of these needs well or badly is not for the
moment to the point. But we take care of these needs not as an
exercise in philanthropy, nor as part of a system or charity, nor as
a last-ditch defense in emergency. We take care of them in consequence of an organized projection of the probable needs of
different categories of individuals, and on the basis of the at least
implicit hypothesis that general social regulation and control are
necessary if these needs are to be served. And it seems to me that
in such arrangements another idea of welfare besides the minimal,
residual concept we have discussed can be discerned—an idea that
is more relevant to the world in which we live. It is a concept of
social welfare whose content would come from forecasting the
needs of individuals in different positions in society, and undertaking, within the limits of available and probable resources, to
provide securely for these needs.

Why should such a concept, an extension of what has been
implicit in much past practice, be systematically adopted as a guide
to welfare policy? Let us recall that we are dealing with a moral
ideal offered as an hypothesis, and let us see what some of its
consequences might be. If we take the so-called "problems of youth"
as examples, welfare, so conceived, would not focus on issues such
as "school drop-outs" or "the prevention of delinquency." Welfare
policy would be based on the recognition that "youth," so-called, is
primarily a social category, a social status, created by law and
convention. The status of "youth" is assigned to all those individuals who, though biologically mature, are nevertheless, for a

variety of reasons, kept in a socially dependent or apprentice position. A transformed concept of welfare would promote inquiry into whether all the reasons normally given for maintaining this state of dependency were justified, the probable categories into which different kinds of "youth" would fall, and the size of the groups concerned—for example, those who would stay in school for ten years, those who would stay for twelve, those who would seek vocational training, those for whom on-the-job training would be best, etc. And it would undertake to provide appropriate environments to meet the needs of all these different categories of young people. Whether the problems of youth would be better dealt with —whether procedures would be more humane, more effective, and, yes, more economical—when approached from this point of view is precisely the hypothesis that would be under examination.

That we have reason to think it an hypothesis worth testing may be suggested by comparing it with our present approach. What this transformed concept of welfare would not encourage would be what, I fear, we mainly do now. This consists, first, in employing definitions that rest more on social ignorance and insularity than on careful inquiry, and which establish some one set of conditions and one type of youth as normal and respectable. It consists, second, in treating those who do not conform to these definitions as special cases calling for philanthropy, therapy, or punishment. It is instructive how quickly, given existing modes of thought, the public mind has come to associate "school drop-out" with "juvenile delinquent" and to regard the former as though it were a mild case of the latter. But the phrase "school drop-out" stands, in general, for a category of person in potential trouble only because there is so little organized social provision, apart from schools, for a large number of young people, who, it can be predicted, will not want to be in school or should not be in school. And I cannot help but note that when such organized provision is not made, the schools themselves are forced to a function not theirs. They become in large part custodial institutions. The deformation of the contemporary school in large cities is a consequence of the purely residual notion of welfare we still employ.

As this example may suggest, the transformed view of welfare

I am describing would presumably have a number of general consequences. It would remove the stigma from welfare. It would
transform welfare from a peripheral function at the fringes of
society to the central object of organized social planning. And it
would turn reflection away from the problem of helping those who
cannot help themselves, and towards the problem of creating conditions in which fewer people will need others' help. The attitude that
now keeps us in a mental bind is reflected in the question which is,
of all questions, the principal one affecting current discussion of
welfare issues. This is the question: How can welfare programmes
be controlled and regulated so that they do not reward shiftlessness,
and do not collide with the primary principle that individuals should
seek to support themselves by work? The question is part and
parcel of the traditional attitude which, on one side, dwells on the
sanctity of work, and, on the other, on the sad necessity for welfare.
It is unlikely that such an approach will be able to deal effectively
with the conditions that make for chronic shiftlessness, and the
inbred disposition to avoid work. The hypothesis implicit in the
concept of welfare that is here proposed is that these problems
would be met more effectively by an approach that focussed not
on punitive sanctions, but on the provision of positive capacities
and motivations to work. This is an essentially long-range process.
It would stress education; it would invite inquiry into the character
and environment of the process of work itself; it would require
creative imagination aimed at organizing work so that it offered to
those who now fear or resent it ampler opportunities for satisfaction
and achievement. Not occupational therapy but the joys of interesting occupation would be at the centre of attention. That there are
limits to what such an approach could accomplish with regard to
making all kinds of work pleasurable goes without saying. But that
it would be more effective in dealing with the problem of voluntary
idleness in an era of abundance than our present methods is surely
an hypothesis worth trying.

Such a concept of welfare, it should be stressed, has a dimension
which the received, residual concept of welfare does not have. The
received concept concentrates on aid to individuals. The transformed concept calls attention as well to social needs. As the

remarks that I have just made may suggest, problems like delinquency, chronic poverty, and unemployment are generally associated with structural deficiencies in the environment of those most affected. They go with inadequate schools, bad health, dispiriting, broken-down neighbourhoods, boredom and its anodyne, violence, and public attitudes of distrust and hostility that every child can detect in the glances of the policeman or the indifference of his teachers.

Problems that also affect the more fortunate members of society —the degrading ugliness and inconvenience of cities, the deterioration of large sections of the countryside, the absence of reasonable opportunities to lift one's intellectual sights if one wishes, the domination of the aesthetic and moral landscape by the art or the craft of the advertiser and the press agent—are problems of a similar sort. They exist in their present degree and intensity because the sector of our economy which is rationalized by the traditional philosophy of free contract has neither the will nor the way to do what is necessary to deal with them. Social needs exist which it is romantic to expect that private enterprise will or can serve. A reasonable balance between the public and private sectors is a prerequisite to the adequate recognition and satisfaction of such general social needs.[4] This is why a transformed and enlarged conception of social welfare—a conception which does not draw its content only from the behaviour of individuals in the market system—is urgently needed, and is, indeed, overdue.

The objections to such a proposed transformation of the ideal of welfare are not hard to imagine. It will be said that it is unrealistic. But the unreality of the traditional conception of welfare, its incapacity to deal with the mounting problems which exist even in terms of its own narrow categories, has, I think, already been demonstrated. Something else has to be tried. It will be said, too, that we can't afford so ambitious an experiment in welfare. But it is doubtful that we can afford less; and most objections on the

[4]Readers of Mr. Galbraith's works will recognize my debt to him in these paragraphs. See especially his recent article, "Economics and the Quality of Life." *Science*, July 10, 1964.

grounds of economy rest on assumptions that stem from the day when the primary item on the human agenda was the struggle against human scarcity. Unless we regard narrow efficiency and pure quantitative productivity as untouchable values, these assumptions have little weight for an era of abundance. And of course it will be said, inevitably, that the transformed conception of welfare that has been presented ignores human motivations by concentrating on the satisfaction of needs rather than on pressures to work, and therefore goes against human nature. But the shift of our economy to its present large-scale corporate form, and its achievement of abundance, has turned into an anachronism the theory of human motivations on which the classic doctrine of maximum work and minimum welfare rested. That theory depended on the assumption that the primitive fear of starvation is an indispensable goad, without which the great unwashed masses of mankind will not work. There has never been much basis for this theory and there is still less today.

Moreover, quite apart from this simplistic theory, human motivations, at any rate in their socially conditioned form, are today undergoing radical changes as a result of changes in the economy. The behaviour of the individual worker at the place of work, for example, is not intelligible as the product of a relation between free individual bargainers and the employer. The individual's relation to the group at the workplace is a cardinal ingredient of his behaviour. It is already plain, furthermore, that the threat of insecurity is not indispensable to motivate the great majority of people who work; and, in any case, the threat is no longer available so far as this great majority is concerned. The incapacity of traditional theories to keep up with such facts, and the inappropriateness of the traditional concept of welfare to them, are among the reasons why the theory and practice of welfare are in their present impasse.

But all this, it will be said—it is the final objection—involves value-judgments, and value-judgments for whose validity no absolute guarantee can be offered. The problem is fundamental, and it is not a purely abstract one. The practical dilemmas to which it points are already becoming visible. The new anti-poverty programmes in the United States, for example, are fairly modest, but they have opened up a variety of issues to which traditional ideas are clearly inappropriate. For if the commitment is undertaken to make a systematic attack on poverty, it turns out fairly quickly that we are attacking a state of affairs that represents a chronic condition of some people. To make a change in this chronic condition requires that some of the deep-seated attitudes of the people concerned be changed. It is not enough simply to arrange a better distribution of opportunity or a more equitable redistribution of wealth, income, and social resources. One must also strive to produce in the people affected a new perception of opportunity and a different evaluation of the uses of wealth, income, and social resources. The problem, therefore, is psychological and cultural; it is what used to be called a moral problem. To deal with it involves using the schools as instruments of re-education; it entails collisions with the home and the family or else the co-opting of them into the process; and it requires a planned attempt to create a physical and social environment that reflects an integrated conception of the type of life towards which men should aspire. All this is to involve the State in programmes that are adventures in moral instruction and reform. And disconcertingly similar problems are present, I cannot help but observe in passing, in much of what we do under the euphemistic name of "technical aid." This is why such programmes give us trouble; and the failure to realize that they are not merely technical programmes, and are not perceived by their recipients as merely technical programmes, is why they give us double trouble.

It is natural enough, then, that there should be serious concern about the expansion of the concept of welfare, and that the view should still exist that it is imperative that we draw a sharp line between the welfare activities in which the State may properly engage and those in which it attempts to redesign a society in the light of a moral vision. "It is essential," says Professor Hayek,

that we become clearly aware of the line that separates a state of affairs in which the community accepts the duty of preventing destitution and of providing a minimum level of welfare from that in which it assumes the power to determine the "just" position of everybody and allocates to each what it thinks he deserves. Freedom is critically threatened when the government is given exclusive powers to provide certain services—powers which, in order to achieve its purpose, it may use for the discretionary coercion of individuals.[5]

But can this sharp line be drawn between an idea of a "minimum level of welfare" and larger conceptions of social justice? The hypothesis that we would do better to adopt a transformed conception of welfare turns on the merits of the arguments pro and con with regard to this issue.

Obviously, no man and no government can say what any individual really deserves, and the thought of drawing up a scale of merit and assigning each person his rightful place in accordance with it would be a form of madness. Nevertheless, a tangle of questionable assumptions is involved, it seems to me, in the notion that a liberal state, bound by the rule of law, can make no substantive judgments about distributive justice, but must accept the results decreed by the impersonal market-place. For it is surely a function of such a state at least to protect the fairness and purity of competition in this market-place. But if that is so, it has to determine, for example, whether monopoly is "fair" and whether labour unions are "fair." It is difficult to see how these judgments can be made on purely procedural grounds. They involve deciding whether or not there are significant inequalities at issue, and whether or not such inequalities should be rectified. This cannot be done purely by appeal to a formal principle of "equality before the law."

The same is true when we consider what must surely be a fundamental function of the liberal state from Professor Hayek's point of view—namely, the safeguarding of the system of free contract. It is only at the boundaries—in relatively exceptional circumstances—that the judicial and executive powers of government are used to enforce contracts between individuals. The State is there to ensure the performance of contracts, but that is not its most normal function. Its more usual function is to make up for human imprevision and inexactness, and for the remarkable capacity of nature and society to produce novel situations that the contracting parties could not have foreseen. To take a simple example, if goods are put on a freight train that never reaches its destination, which

[5]F. V. Hayek, *The Constitution of Liberty* (Chicago: University of Chicago Press, 1960), pp. 289–90.

of the contracting parties shall take the loss—the seller or the buyer? In such ambiguous or unforeseen circumstances, where the contract itself offers no answer, the courts have to decide what constitutes performance, and how the burdens accruing to non-performance shall be distributed. In effect, the courts are deciding how the risks incident to contracts shall be distributed. If this can be done without appeal to substantive notions of distributive justice, some wholly unforeseen changes in the laws of logic have taken place.

Similar considerations apply to the notion that a liberal government will not take it upon itself to be the moral arbiter of the community. If a free society exists, the government will surely not be the only arbiter. But it cannot escape being an arbiter, and an influential one, whatever its view of welfare. Liberal states engage in education; they encourage patriotism; they honour noble men; and even when they are neutral with regard to religion, they generally give religious establishments indirect subsidies by exempting them from taxation. All of these would seem to involve value-judgments. There is, indeed, a certain disingenuousness in the argument that political officials have no right to impose their personal moral or aesthetic preferences on others. The argument suggests that nobody else is making the attempt. But the effort to cut the tastes of the citizenry to the pattern of one's own tastes—or, at any rate, one's own economic advantage—is a major industry in modern societies and absorbs a good part of the national wealth.

Nor is it true that governments that restrict themselves to a minimal conception of welfare do not engage in the discretionary coercion of individuals. In many parts of the United States, intrusions into private life including midnight visits by officials on private citizens are normal elements in the supervision and enforcement of welfare laws. These invasions of the privacy of the poor constitute one of the most widespread and serious threats to the right to privacy with which we are now confronted. Yet they are commonly condoned by precisely those people who argue that any enlargement of the conception of welfare beyond relief from destitution entails grave threats to private rights, and threatens the growth of a moralistic, Big Brotherly officialdom. Our welfare activities, under their existing rationale, are in fact wholly governed by an antecedent moral ideal. Their intent is to encourage people to wish to work and to live decently. I could not agree with that intent more wholeheartedly. I permit myself some reservations, however, about the effectiveness of the pedagogical methods that are employed, and about their congruences with regard to the protection of elementary rights that all citizens of free societies should presumably possess.

In sum, there would be more force to the charge that an enlarged welfare state must necessarily impose a special moral vision on the citizenry if those who made the objection could themselves plead innocent to the charge. But if the arguments I offered in my first lecture have any validity, we have already seen that the concept of welfare which treats welfare as a matter of relief from destitution, and attempts to extrude all questions of a larger social justice, nevertheless makes some considerable moral commitments. It reflects and accepts certain definite ways of recruiting and rewarding labour, certain definite arrangements for the distribution of the penalties and rewards of economic production, and certain unmistakably class-angled views about the moral obligations to earn one's living by the sweat of one's brow. The conception of social justice that emerges from these commitments may not always be either articulate or defensible, but it is a conception of social justice just the same.

But I would add a most important cautionary note. If there is confusion on this side, there should not be a parallel error on the other. It is an hypothesis that the conception of welfare I have adumbrated could be adopted as a programme of action without sacrificing fundamental liberties. That hypothesis should not be certified a priori by playing tricks with words. What gives pause to partisans of liberty when they contemplate the enlargement of the ideal of welfare is a point of view that has become increasingly widespread. It consists in the total identification of welfare and freedom. The adoption of this way of thinking is ruinous to the conception of welfare within freedom for which I am attempting to make a case.

It is tempting to think that "welfare" is really all that we can seriously mean by "freedom." In a famous passage in *Equality*, Tawney wrote:

There is no such thing as freedom in the abstract, divorced from the realities of a particular time and place. Whatever else the conception may imply, it involves a power of choice between alternatives, a choice which is real, not merely nominal, between alternatives which exist in fact, not only on paper. . . . It means the ability to do, or to refrain from doing, definite things, at a definite moment, in definite circumstances, or it means nothing at all.

The intent of this argument is both clear and laudable. If young Peter is free to attend any school of his choice in the sense that the law says he may and promises to support him against anyone who tries to prevent him from doing so, but if there simply is no school within fifty miles of his home, Peter's freedom is an abstraction and it is a cruel joke to tell him that he has the right to choose his school. To give freedom meaning and substance it has to be associated with power and opportunity. Otherwise, it is a mere formalism, an empty, indeed a cynical, word. There is a long tradition, which includes liberal philosophers from T. H. Green to John Dewey, that has taken this view. Indeed, the tendency to see welfare as an integral part of freedom has been enshrined in the Atlantic Charter, which places "freedom from want" among the four freedoms. Still, despite its distinguished intellectual pedigree, this view of freedom spreads confusion. It mixes up quite distinguishable things. "Freedom" and "welfare" both stand for desirable goals of human endeavour, but they are not the same goal. I have freedom when, in a given situation, no man or law prevents or prohibits me from doing a given thing if I wish to do it. My welfare is something else—it is a matter of my physical and mental health, of the resources at my disposal, of my powers and opportunities.

Of course, there is very often little or no value in my possessing a freedom unless I have the ability and opportunity to act on it. But this does not mean that the ability and opportunity are the same as the freedom. I may have the ability and opportunity to study, to travel, or to refute the nonsense I hear from the leaders of governments, but I may still not have the freedom to do any of these things. And if it is true that the ability and opportunity to do something is generally necessary if the freedom to do it is to be important to a man, the reverse is also true: with regard to a great many things, the freedom to do them is necessary if the ability and opportunity to do them are to emerge.

To be sure, Tawney, in the statement I have quoted, speaks of freedom as "the ability to do or to refrain from doing," and thereby indicates that he thinks there can be no freedom without choice. Still, it is important from the point of view of social policy to keep clearly separate the question whether a man has the ability and opportunity to do something and the question whether he has the freedom to do it. Otherwise we may find ourselves saying odd things such as that the citizens of Country X are freer than they used to be because they have more medical care these days. It ought to be possible at least to raise the question whether there is a conflict between better medical care and freedom. To do this we have to avoid defining our terms so that the question is answered a priori.

Indeed, the habit of identifying welfare and freedom can lead us to say, as many have indeed said, that we are really free precisely when, and only when, we have reached a stage of such utter well-being and moral self-realization that it does not occur to us ever to want to do anything that we ought not to do. It is intelligible that there should be a long tradition, going back to Saint Paul and beyond, in which people speak of freedom in this way. Most of us know what it is to struggle against irresolution or plain laziness, against inner divisions and constraints, against odd blockages inside us, or against perverse drives to do what, soberly, we would not wish to do. And in such circumstances, we often speak quite naturally of wishing somehow to be "free." We mean that we wish to be whole, to be in unimpeded command of ourselves, and it is natural to call this state "freedom" because if we were whole, if we were in command of ourselves, we should have got rid of these strange drives and restraints and weaknesses that we feel are somehow external to our real selves, and that do not belong with what we are and are trying to be. And from this it is very easy to move on, and to say that we are not our real selves when we are tempted to do wrong, or when, in our blindness, we choose the wrong only because we did not know the right. And then freedom becomes the same thing as complete moral well-being. It is nothing but our welfare, full and complete.

This way of speaking about "freedom" dissolves freedom into welfare. To the extent that we adopt it, we must be prepared to grant to the State, or to whatever institution knows what is really good for us, supreme and unchallenged authority to promote our well-being. But the satisfaction of our needs, even our highest needs, is not freedom unless we retain the right to choose, including the right to make the wrong choices. It is possible—it is necessary—to say that freedom of choice is an integral part of what we shall choose to mean by "the good life"; it is not possible, without dire confusion, to say that freedom is nothing more than our welfare.

Accordingly, in suggesting that any conception of human welfare has a moral bias written into it, and in urging that the State undertake a commitment to human welfare just the same, I have very much in mind a necessary limiting condition. I should not wish liberal governments to adopt the broad conception of welfare that I have described if they were the only centres of power or the only sources of employment and benefits in the community. If they were the only centres of power in the community, indeed, they would not be liberal states. For the older conception of welfare that I have rejected nevertheless performed an indispensable function. It served as a support of a philosophy that put individual choice at the centre of the stage, and that helped guide and regulate the struggle in the West to free individuals from irrevocable dependence on any particular group. The assumption that there will be choice, that a pluralistic society will exist and that individuals will have some opportunity to say "yes" or "no" where official notions of human welfare are concerned, is central to what I have said.

The transformed concept of welfare thus retains an essential element of the older concept. Its heart is the right to choose. It merely goes further than the older concept in its concern for freedom. It proposes to ensure that the beneficiaries of welfare measures have not only the right but the intelligent power to choose. That, it seems to me, is what "welfare," in the end, is all about. It stands for the effort to create a society in which individuals will have significant choices, and will have sufficient knowledge and ability and resources so that, when they make the choices, they can reasonably be held responsible for what they have done.

Is it possible for governments to undertake so large a responsibility without becoming tyrannical? It is possible, I think, though it is obvious that we should not take the safety of freedom for granted. There is much that should legitimately concern us in the growth of so many bureaus, forms, regulations, committees, and committees to co-ordinate committees, and in the steady increase in the number of official and semi-official interventions in daily and personal life. However, there is no evidence that a conscious moral vision is the cause of this state of affairs. On the contrary, all this has come about in the absence of order and plan, and may well be its product. We ought at least to examine the alternative possibility that organized planning directed by a co-ordinated idea of welfare could reduce the daily weight and cost of the governmental presence.

In practice, then, an enlightened public welfare policy need not consist in the coercive imposition on a community of a point of view. It need not consist in this even where it concerns itself explicitly, as I believe it should, with aesthetic issues or with the protection and projection of standards of taste and achievement cherished only by a minority. Such a policy is simply an effort to restore perspective and balance; it is an effort to ensure that the better will not suffer because few know that it exists. For you cannot be said to know what you are choosing unless you know the alternatives, and there is no way of escaping Philistia unless you know there are other countries. A decent amplitude of genuine choice for all citizens is a reasonable and necessary objective of liberal government. I am inclined to think that in this objective we sum up most of what we mean by "welfare."